Future Studies

in the K-12 Curriculum

by

John D. Haas

#19101701

Social Science Education Consortium
Boulder, Colorado
1988

Second Edition

ORDERING INFORMATION

This publication is available from:

Social Science Education Consortium, Inc.
855 Broadway
Boulder, Colorado 80302

ISBN 0-89994-324-1

CONTENTS

PREFACE

One of the dilemmas faced by teachers and curriculum developers in such broad fields as language arts, science, and social studies is how to incorporate into these already-crowded curricula new timely topics and crucial current social issues. Probably the dilemma will always be present, since the curriculum is constantly in a state of dynamic equilibrium between the forces of continuity and change. Perhaps all curricular subjects should include both traditional topics and current topics, the old and the new, the esoteric and the relevant.

In advocating a place for future studies in the curriculum, I do not have in mind any magic model or special slot. A modest beginning is all that one can expect: a few lessons, a short unit, a course here and there; an interested and enterprising teacher or coordinator in this school or that district. Monumental changes may not be possible in American public education, but infiltration strategies by individuals and small groups can be successful. This is how the futures movement achieved its beginnings, and also how future studies emerged in schools and colleges. Perhaps grand designs should be suspect.

Many claims can be and have been made for the inclusion of future studies in the curriculum. Five are particularly persuasive for me:

1. Because children and youth have the greatest portion of the future available to them.

2. Because the time continuum is incomplete without the future to extend the past and present.

3. Because citizens need to be participants in decisions that affect their collective future.

4. Because individuals need to envision their personal goals as motivational spurs to action and achievement.

5. Because we all need to perceive the generations of our species not yet born in order to be stewards for them.

This monograph was written for teachers and curriculum developers who have some interest in planning units and courses on the future. Since the study of the future is multidisciplinary in nature, the units and courses might be in any subject, but are probably most appropriate in language arts, science, or social studies. The reader should know, however, that this author's background is mainly in social studies. Further, the reader should be aware that this is neither a step-by-step curriculum primer nor a collection of responses to the question, "What do I do Monday?"

The volume was written to accomplish two goals: (1) to provide a brief introduction to the field of futurology (especially human social futures), which occupies almost three-fourths of the book, and (2) to offer some suggestions for teaching future studies in elementary and secondary schools, including potential topics and course and unit formats. The monograph ends with three bibliographies that should be useful to readers who wish to pursue various topics in more depth.

A final caveat! Though I am not a professional futurist, I do have a preference for the Transformationalist point of view as contrasted with that of the Extrapolationist, which is to say I tend to agree with those futurists who see the need to abandon (or at least to modify) those values and assumptions of Western industrialized nations that have brought these societies to the brink of disaster and that threaten the future existence of our species. I am gravely alarmed, yet hopeful for the needed transformations in culture and consciousness. This is not the dominant view among futurists.

Now there is one outstanding important fact regarding Spaceship Earth, and that is that no instruction book came with it... Thus, because the instruction manual was missing we are learning how we safely can anticipate the consequence of an increasing number of alternative ways of extending our satisfactory survival and growth—both physical and metaphysical.

Fuller, R. B. *Operating Manual for Spaceship Earth*. New York: Pocket Books, 1970, pp. 47-48.

Time, said St. Augustine, is a three-fold present: the present as we experience it, the past as a present memory, and the future as a present expectation.

Bell, D. "The year 2000—the trajectory of an idea." *Daedalus*, Vol. 96, No. 3 (Summer 1967), p. 639.

ACKNOWLEDGMENTS

We would like to thank the following publishers and authors for permission to use material appearing on the following pages:

Page v: Daniel Bell and the estate of R. Buckminster Fuller.

Pages 5-6: excerpts from *World Economic Development*. Reprinted by permission of Westview Press from *World Economic Development*, by Herman Kahn. Copyright 1979 by Westview Press, Boulder, Colorado.

Pages 10-11: excerpts from *Megatrends*. Copyright 1982 by John Naisbitt. Reprinted with permission of Warner Books, New York.

Page 13: excerpts from *Unfinished Animal*, by Theodore Roszak. Copyright 1975 by Theodore Roszak. Reprinted by permission of Harper and Row, Publishers, Inc.

Pages 16-18: excerpts from *New Rules*, by Daniel Yankelovich. Copyright 1981. Reprinted by permission of Random House, Inc.

Pages 18-20: tables and figure on Values and Lifestyles. Reprinted with permission of Macmillan Publishing Company from *The Nine American Lifestyles*, by Arnold Mitchell. Copyright 1983.

Page 29: drawing reprinted with permission from *The Futurist,* published by the World Future Society.

Page 42: graph. Reprinted with permission of Macmillan Publishing Company from *World Facts and Trends*, by John McHale. Copyright 1972 by John McHale.

Page 43: excerpt from *Seven Tomorrows*, by Paul Hawken, James Ogilvy, and Peter Schwartz. Copyright 1982. Permission to reprint requested from Bantam Books.

Page 45: futures wheel. Reprinted by permission of ERIC/CAPS, University of Michigan.

Page 47: cross-impact matrix. Reprinted with permission from *The Futurist*, published by the World Future Society, 4916 Saint Elmo Avenue, Bethesda, MD 20814.

Page 50: description of the Delphi technique from *The Futurists*. Reprinted by permission of Albert Somit.

Page 64: guidelines for teachers. Adapted from *Futurism and Future Studies*, copyright 1980, National Education Association. Reprinted with permission of NEA.

Pages 67-68: learning objectives. Reprinted from *Teaching the Future*, copyright 1976, with the permission of ETC Publications, Palm Springs, CA 92263-1608.

Pages 71-72: goals for futures education. Reprinted from *Futures Unlimited*, pp. 85-86, with permission of the National Council for the Social Studies.

Pages 75-76: table of contents from *Visions of the Future*, a textbook on the past, present, and future. Copyright 1984 by the Hudson Institute. Reprinted by permission of the publisher.

1. INTRODUCTION

We are all time travelers, able to journey at will through past and future landscapes, and all this by virtue of a most remarkable time machine within each of our heads. Time-bound in one sense, in another we're able to create time-warps, which speed us in an instant to strange or familiar habitats, past or future, within or outside the universe. In our genes, in our collective unconscious, in our experiences, each of us *is* a universe, a time-space of unique dimensions.

The future is one of our natural abodes. Not only can we dwell there, we can create what *is* there. As in all of our many existences, in our futures we are both creatures and creators. To know our futures as much as to know our pasts is to know ourselves. In the invisible interval, at that point in motion, we exist. And it is the *quality* of our existence that concerns us most as we probe our possible futures.

Human beings have never been strangers to the future. A few million years ago our ancestors already comprehended nature's cycles: day and night, life and death, and the tell-tale signs of the seasons—occurrence and recurrence. Ancient oracles, prophets, and seers were futurists, as were astronomers and naturalists. But more important, *all* humans are futurists because we care—about ourselves, our children, our friends, our species. Because we care, we choose—to reproduce, to nurture, to protect, to secure, to create, or even not to choose and to submit to the fates. To live and to value life is our supreme commitment to the future.

Origins of Modern Futures Movement

For almost the entire span of existence of *Homo sapiens*, change in the conditions of our survival has been relatively slow.

> The fewer changes we anticipate, the more we can continue to rely on our knowledge for the future....On the other hand, the future validity of our knowledge becomes increasingly doubtful as the mood of society inclines toward change and the changes promise to be more rapid.[1]

It was in such a time of social turmoil, the mid-1960s, that the modern professional futures movement catapulted into prominence on the global scene. Its contemporary origins, however, can be traced to the era of World War II. At that time the military became concerned about the prospects of new weapons, and the term they used to describe future developments in weaponry was "technological forecasting." After the war,

> scientists and the military, impressed by the way in which such radically new scientific and technological break-throughs as radar, the atomic bomb, and intercontinental ballistic missiles had transformed warfare, began to search on a regular basis for ways in which the nature of the next war could be predicted and planned for in advance.[2]

The now-famous Rand Corporation had its beginnings as a military "futures shop" in the 1940s. Most of the other futures organizations in the United States, however, were founded between 1959 and 1976. For example, the Cambridge Research Institute, Inc. (Cambridge, MA) was founded in 1959; Society for the Investigation of Recurring Events (Linden, NJ) in 1960; the Hudson Institute (Croton-on-Hudson, NY) in 1961; the World Future Society (Washington, DC) in 1966; Stanford Research Institute's Center for the Study of Social Policy (Menlo Park, CA) and Educational Policy Research Center (Syracuse, NY) in 1967; the Institute for the Future (Menlo Park, CA) in 1968; Futuremics, Inc. (Washington, DC) and The Futures Groups, Inc. (Glastonbury, CT) in 1971; the Office of Technology Assessment of the U.S. Congress (Washington, DC) in 1973; the Worldwatch Institute (Washington, DC) in 1974; the Congressional Clearinghouse on the Future (Washington, DC) in 1976. Worldwide, several hundred corporations, institutes, associations, and public agencies are dedicated to the study of the future.

Some Key Futures Concepts

The Futures Field. The names applied to the field that encompasses the study of the future have created some confusion. Probably the four most recognized terms in this field are "future studies," "futurology," "futurism," and "futuristics." When the focus is on social policy decisions, the term used is "policy research"; the term "technology assessment" applies to concerns about new technological inventions, products, or processes. There is general agreement, however, that practitioners of the art/science of studying the future are "futurists."

The term "future studies" is often used when referring to the study of the future as a part of school curricula, usually in the broad curricular fields of English, science, or social studies, or in multi-disciplinary courses.

A related source of some debate has to do with what term is appropriate for describing the outcomes of futures research. Usually, futurists avoid using words like "prediction" and "prophecy." "Prediction" implies a control of phenomena and a precision in measurement more suited to the physical sciences and their use of experimental methods than to futurology and its phenomena and conditions. On the other hand, futurists also are reluctant to use the word "prophecy" because of its traditional connection with religious prophets or fortune-telling charlatans. The preferred term is "forecast" (and "forecasting") because this term suggests the *probability* of future events or phenomena, as in the forecasts of meteorologists. Futurology is considered to be a blend of science and art.

The Time Dimension. The word "future" is one of three quite general terms applied to time, the other two being "past" and "present." Of course, these are human constructs, terms of convenience. Time is a dimension of existence, a continuum that is relative to place, context, and observer. It is common practice, nevertheless, to speak of humans' perceptions of time as extending backward from now, the present, into a past of experienced and vicarious events—and forward from now into a future of possible or probable, sought and hoped for or to-be-avoided "events." Thus, in the sense that events can occur in a past or a future, there can be a history of the future as well as of the past.

With respect to "time in the future," futurists generally use a number of time-frame conceptions. These are:[3]

1. The "immediate" future is now.

2. The "near-term" future is the next one to five years.

3. The "middle-range" future is five to twenty years from now.

4. The "long-range" future occurs twenty to fifty years hence.

5. The "far" future will happen fifty years or more from now.

Another aspect of the temporal dimension is the great disparity between the time of a generation in a human family (about 30 years) or of a person's lifetime (about 70 years in the United States) *and* time in the universe or in our particular solar system, which is measured in millions and billions of Earth years. How does one gain perspective on one's own life expectancy or that of one's children or grandchildren in comparison with the age of the Sun—10,000,000,000 years, or of Earth—5,000,000,000 years, or of the human species—perhaps 3,000,000 years? Such differences in micro time and macro time are extremely difficult if not almost impossible to comprehend.

The Global Concept. As Buckminster Fuller so aptly put it: "We are all astronauts!"[4] What Fuller meant, of course, is that Earth is a spaceship in a relatively fixed orbit around our Sun-star, our "energy-supplying mother-ship." We, the passengers aboard Earth-ship, are "right now traveling at 60,000 miles an hour around the Sun," while at the same time we are "also spinning axially, which, at the latitude of Washington, D.C., adds approximately 1,000 miles per hour to our motion. Each minute we both spin at 100 miles and zip in orbit at 1,000 miles."[5]

Those magnificent photographs of Earth taken by astronauts aboard NASA space vehicles gave us our first views of our spherical planet *as a whole*, as a total system, as Spaceship Earth. What was beautifully clear from those technicolor enlargements was a planetary landscape devold of political boundaries—a multicolored spheroid looking very much like a gigantic microorganism on a slide beneath the high-powered lens of a microscope. Organism is an appropriate metaphor, for Earth is not only a complete biosphere, but it is also dependent for existence on its Sun-host as a source of sustaining gravitation, energy, and light.

We have just recently become aware of the interdependence that exists among Earth's several hundred human societies, another key concept related to a global perspective.

> When we talk about such things as the Shrinking Planet, or Spaceship Earth, or the Global Village, we are acknowledging the fact that the human species is being more tightly bound together with each passing day. We find ourselves living in huge global webs, although awareness often comes only when some sudden jolt in one of the strands—like the Energy Crisis—reverberates through all the others.[6]

To emphasize planetwide interdependence as a key concept in futurology is not meant to suggest that futurists have no interest in such smaller social units as a single nation, a city or town, or even a local corporation. The reason for a global focus is that social issues, as manifest in any locale, are more and more interwoven within and between societies. Social futures must therefore take into account global contexts.

The Concept of Planning. Humankind seems always to be ambivalent toward social change. Philosophical issues often are stated as dilemmas: free will vs. determinism (or predestination), personal freedom vs. social control, disjointed incrementalism vs. long-range social planning. It becomes a question of to choose or not to choose, to set goals or to submit to the fates, to plan or not to plan for the future.

Futurists tend to accept the assumption to a greater or lesser degree that individuals, communities, and societies are free to choose among alternative futures. Thus, futurists believe that personal or social choices can be made, even though within severely restricted limits, and that these preferred options have future consequences. They further believe that the selection process should be rational in nature, that is, that selection of a preferred future should be reached through comparative analysis of a range of scenarios or alternative future contexts. Futurists accept, however, that an intimate aspect of every choice is the normative or value dimension. To choose a set of goals and attendant probable consequences (from among several such sets) is not solely a rational enterprise, but is value-laden at every point.

Making choices among alternatives and setting goals and priorities are inescapable facets of futurism and components of the general process of planning. Applied futurology, then, is the development and pursuit of planned social change. Planning is a form of rational decision making, based on value premises, with a hopeful attitude toward the future, and is partly, if not wholly, anti-fatalistic.

Self-fulfilling and Self-defeating Forecasts. We are not totally at the mercy of a predetermined future. We are able to describe alternative futures and then choose those futures we desire and work toward their achievement. Conversely, we can identify those futures we do not want to occur and work for their defeat. Thus, as both creatures and creators of futures, we can identify and specify alternative futures and then choose which ones to support or oppose.

Two phenomena connected with the specification of probable futures are "self-fulfilling" and "self-defeating" psychological forces. For example, to highlight a probable shortfall of petroleum to process into gas and oil for automobiles may tend to "cause" or "create," at least in part, just such a shortage.

In such a case, the actual forecast of an event becomes a partial cause of bringing it about—a self-ful-filling forecast. If we know in detail the probable horrors of thermonuclear war, for example, this awareness may become a self-defeating "cause" that will prevent the occurrence of such an event.

Orientations to the Future

There are many attitudes toward and points of view about the future. Futurists are a curious blend of colors and shades: cautious and starry-eyed optimists; fatalistic and realistic pessimists; eschatologists (religionists who prophecy or study endings); cornucopians (optimists who see a horn of plenty for all) and catastrophists (who see crisis upon crisis); utopians and their opposite, dystopians; and extrapolationists (who view the future as a continuation of past-to-present trends), transitionists (who anticipate slow, significant change over generations or centuries), and transformationists (who forecast rapid, dramatic, traumatic, revolutionary change). These last three types—extrapolationists, transitionists, and transformationists—can be arrayed on a continuum that extends from continuity or minimal change at one end to perpetual, rapid, or revolutionary change at the opposite extreme (Figure 1).

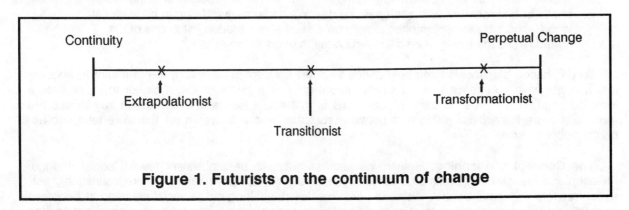

Figure 1. Futurists on the continuum of change

Extrapolationist. In one sense all futurists are extrapolationists, since to extrapolate means to estimate an unknown based on known facts and data. We, however, are using the term to describe those futurists who view the future as a continuation of past-to-present dominant trends. For this group, the past-to-present time frame varies from 500 years (since 1500—the end of the Middle Ages in Europe), to 100 years (since about 1880—the Industrial Revolution era in the United States), to the post-World War II period in Europe, Japan, and North America.

The prototype nation or society for the extrapolationist is one that is highly industrialized, urbanized, and technology-driven such as Japan, West Germany, or the United States. By "trickle-down" or "exportation," the rest of the world's nations will follow the lead of these "advanced" examples of modernization. For the extrapolationist, talk of "limits" is a defeatist attitude, while sustained economic growth is the ideal, synonymous with progress.

The extrapolationist is an optimist and a cornucopian, one who believes in Western civilization and its cultural and material benefits, especially the standard of living provided by capitalism, industrialism, and scientific/technological developments. A flavor of this viewpoint comes through the following quote from a special issue on the future in *U.S. News and World Report* (May 9, 1983):

> What lies ahead could well be a renaissance for the U.S. in political prestige and technological power. People will live to a healthy old age of 100 or more, as superdrugs cure diseases such as cancer and senility. Genetic techniques will expand food production and curb pollution. Space colonies will orbit the earth, and the moon will be mined for its wealth. Robots will do household and factory chores, and cars will be programmed to avoid accidents...With home computers and other electronic marvels, families will tap into enormous sources of data and entertainment. As the revolution in

high technology gains momentum, an economic boom will give tomorrow's citizens the highest standard of living ever known.[7]

Two of those futurists who appear to fit the extrapolationist mold are the late Herman Kahn (*The Year 2000*, with A. J. Wiener, 1967; *The Next 200 Years*, with others, 1976; *World Economic Development*, 1979; *The Coming Boom*, 1982); and Gerard K. O'Neill (*The High Frontier: Human Colonies in Space*, 1977; *2081: A Hopeful View of the Human Future*, 1981).

Herman Kahn is probably best known as the director of the Hudson Institute (Croton-on-Hudson, NY), a futures "shop" he founded after leaving the Rand Corporation (Santa Monica, CA). As a futurist, he propounded a continuity scheme he called "The Basic Long-Term Multifold Trend of Western Culture," a pattern or complex of interrelated trends that began about 1500 and is characterized by the concept of progress.[8]

Kahn argued that the Multifold Trend:

> is best thought of as a single entity whose every aspect is both a cause and an effect — a driving force and a consequence. [The elements] should be thought of as aspects or parts of a whole. The Multifold Trend affects every aspect and part of society: fine arts, truth systems, family relationships, government, performing arts, architecture, ethics and morality, music, law, economics, civic relationships, literature, and education.[9]

The Trend is further explained in Table 1. One should note that item 13 suggests that the 12 trends will spread to the less developed nations, thus making the Trend a global phenomenon; and that 14 anticipates that the tempo at which each preceding trend occurs will accelerate until a peak is reached.

Gerard K. O'Neill, a Princeton physics professor, has been most associated with the idea and feasibility of space colonies. For him the new frontier is space exploration and colonization, what he refers to as "the high frontier."[10] He reveals his viewpoint in this quote from his popular book, *2081*:

> But in every type of futuristic writing, from the impersonal to the subjective, I found the same pattern: most prophets overestimated how much the world would be transformed by social and political change and underestimated the forces of technological change.[11]

In a major section (II) of *2081*, he identifies five of what he calls "drivers of change." These are "developments that [he] believes will determine, alone and in combination, the course of the next hundred years."[12] The five are: (1) computers, (2) automation, (3) space colonies, (4) energy, and (5) communications.[13]

O'Neill expects the microcomputer to be able to store more in less space and to manipulate data faster:

> Long before 2081, perhaps even in this century, it will be possible to store in a machine the size of a business card all the information in a good-sized library. That will help to bring about a reduction in the scale of institutions — what one might call 'social miniaturization.'[14]

For automation he has in mind the expanded uses of computers in industrial applications such as the computer-controlled welding machines used today in most automobile factories. Beyond the single automated machine is the totally automated factory, and then comes the self-replicating machine that is capable of reproducing itself.[15]

O'Neill's favorite solution for most current problems is the space colony, which will free Earth's population from the many forms of troublesome limits and scarcities: territory, energy, food, clean air and water, and size of population. He sees space colonies as a means of moving from "an economics

Table 1
The Basic Long-Term Multifold Trend[16]

Some aspects of this trend go back a thousand years; except as noted, most go back several centuries. This trend is toward:

1. **Increasingly Sensate Culture** (empirical, this-worldly, secular, humanistic, pragmatic, manipulative, explicitly rational, utilitarian, contractual, epicurean, hedonistic, etc.) — recently, an almost complete decline of the sacred and of "irrational" taboos, charismas, and authority structures

2. **Accumulation of Scientific and Technological Knowledge** — recently, an emergence of a genuine theoretical framework for the biological sciences; but social sciences are still in an early, largely empirical, and idealistic state

3. **Institutionalization of Technological Change**, especially research, development, innovation, and diffusion — recently a conscious emphasis on finding and creating synergisms and serendipities

4. **Increasing Role of Bourgeois, Bureaucratic, "Meritocratic" Elites** — recently, an emergence of intellectual and technocratic elites as a class; increasing literacy and education for everyone; the "knowledge industry" and "triumph" of theoretical knowledge

5. **Increasing Military Capability of Western Cultures** — recently, the issues of mass destruction, terrorism, and diffusion of advanced military technologies (both nuclear and conventional) to non-Western cultures

6. **Increasing Area of World Dominated or Greatly Influenced by Western Culture** — but recently, the West is becoming more reticent; a consequent emphasis on synthesis with indigenous cultures and various "ethnic" revivals

7. **Increasing Affluence** — and recently, more stress on egalitarianism

8. **Increasing Rate of World Population Growth** — until recently, this rate has probably passed its zenith, or soon will

9. **Urbanization** — and recently, suburbanization and "urban sprawl," soon the growth of megalopoli, "sun belts," and rural areas with urban infrastructure and amenities

10. **Increasing Recent Attention to Macroenvironmental Issues** (e.g., constraints set by finiteness of Earth and limited capacity of various local and global reservoirs to accept pollution)

11. **Decreasing Importance of Primary and, Recently, Secondary Occupations** — soon a similar decline in tertiary occupations and an increasing emphasis on advanced, honorific, or desirable quaternary occupations and activities

12. **Emphasis on "Progress" and Future-Oriented Thinking, Discussion, and Planning** — recently, some retrogression in the technical quality of such activities; conscious and planned innovation and manipulative rationality (e.g., social engineering) increasingly applied to social, political, cultural, and economic worlds, as well as to shaping and exploiting the material world; increasing role of ritualistic, incomplete or pseudo-rationality

13. **Increasing Universality of the Multifold Trend**

14. **Increasing Tempo of Change in All the Above** (which may, however, soon peak in many areas)

of scarcity...to an economics of abundance... Once we break out from the confines of the planet, we can begin building new lands from the limitless resources of our solar system..."[17] When can we build such colonies as human-made Earth satellites? O'Neill concludes that the knowledge and technology to build a hundred square mile colony is now "within the limits of known engineering practice."[18] The price tag, however, would place such a project only within the realm of a many-nation effort.

The fourth driver of change is energy, and O'Neill expects that progress on many fronts simultaneously—nuclear (fusion and breeder reactors), improved, energy-efficient modes of transportation, liquid hydrogen, Earth-based solar, and conservation—will solve the short-term problem. But for the twenty-first century, his preference is Satellite Solar Power, solar energy captured on a space satellite and relayed as low-density microwaves to Earth.[19]

Finally, O'Neill argues that global communication needs can be met by larger satellites with larger antennas and more powerful transmitters, which in turn will allow for smaller, cheaper ground equipment on Earth. For education, shopping, and business, communication technologies will obviate the need to do much travel from home. What will make this feasible are computers, communication satellites, fiber optic cables, and criss-crossing networks.[20]

Transitionist. The transitionist perspective is one of gradual change over a time period of centuries or even millenia. The change, however, unlike change for the extrapolationist, is qualitative and pervasive, a demarcation between two differing ways of life, rather than a blending of events in an inexorable flow. Thus, a transitionist talks about transitional change: *from* "X" *to* "Y" or *from* epoch (or era) "A" *to* epoch "B" or *from* industrial society *to* postindustrial society.

Jonas Salk illustrates the "from/to" evolutionary change that exemplifies the transitionist orientation. He argues that today we are at a transition point, a watershed, between two societal patterns. We are moving from Epoch A (past-to-present) to Epoch B (present-to-future). "A" is characterized by exponential growth; whereas "B" is captured in the concept of dynamic stability. The two types, "A" and "B", are juxtaposed, as in Figure 2.[21] Salk describes this double curve as a sigmoid or S-like curve.

Epochs A and B, according to Salk, differ along several dimensions, as shown in Table 2.

Two futurists who typify the transitionist mode are Daniel Bell (*Toward the Year 2000*, 1967; *The Coming of Post-Industrial Society*, 1973; *The Cultural Contradictions of Capitalism*, 1976) and John Naisbitt (*Megatrends*, 1982).

Along with Kenneth Boulding, Daniel Bell has popularized the term and concept, "postindustrial society." Bell posits three forms of society: preindustrial, industrial, and postindustrial. Each has an origin, a peak time, and a period of decline. As can be seen in Figure 3, the preindustrial societies began at the earliest about 10,000 B.C., while it is difficult to find many societies of this type today. The origins of industrial society occur during the time preindustrial societies are the dominant mode. The invention of the horse collar might be considered a beginning of industrial society, while the period between World Wars I and II in the U.S. might mark its peak. Although nations in Eurasia and North America have achieved the fullest development of industrial society, many nations of Africa and Asia have not yet made the transition from the preindustrial to the industrial stage.

During the nineteenth century, crude forms of linotype, typewriters, and mechanical calculators appeared, and these signal the origins of postindustrial society. Today, the transition to post-industrial society has been made by the United States, the Soviet Union, Eastern and Western European nations, Canada, and Japan.

What are the chief characteristics of each of the three societal types? Bell summarizes these in Table 3, by reference to four categories: Resource, Mode, Technology, and Design. The main resources used by humans in preindustrial societies are such raw materials as berries, nuts, grubs, minerals, roots, wild grains, and numerous varieties of animals. Even agriculture and the domestication of animals

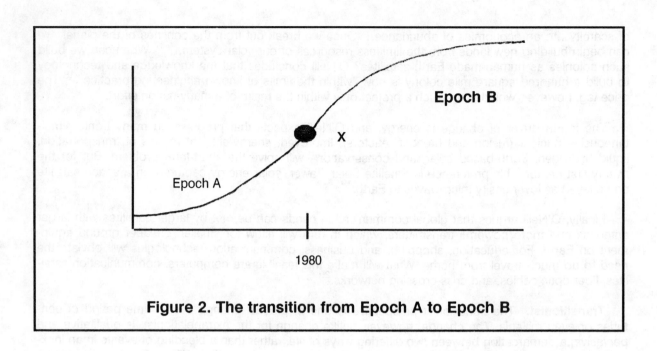

Figure 2. The transition from Epoch A to Epoch B

Table 2
Differences Between Epochs A and B

Epoch A	Epoch B
1. Strong Ego—dominance of intellect and will	1. Integration of "Being" and Ego
2. Anti-Death	2. Prolife
3. Anti-Disease	3. Prohealth
4. Death Control	4. Birth Control
5. Self-Repression	5. Self-Expression
6. External Restraints	6. Self-Restraint
7. Human-Over-Nature Ethic	7. Ecological Ethic

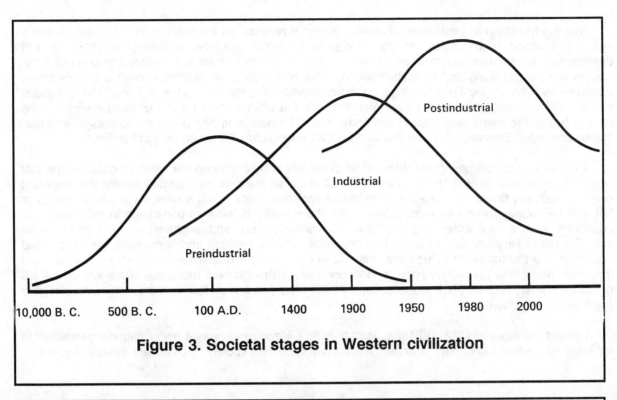

Figure 3. Societal stages in Western civilization

Preindustrial

Industrial

Postindustrial

10,000 B. C.   500 B. C.   100 A.D.   1400   1900   1950   1980   2000

	Preindustrial	Industrial	Postindustrial
Resource	Raw Materials	Energy	Information
Mode	Extraction	Fabrication	Processing
Technology	Labor-Intensive	Capital-Intensive	Knowledge-Intensive
Design	Game Against Nature	Game Against Fabricated Nature	Game Between Persons

Table 3
Characteristics of Bell's Three Societal Types[22]

are reserved to pre-industrial society. The major "industries" are agriculture, mining, fishing, and forestry, all powered by raw human or animal energy. The design is a game against relentless natural forces—how to merely survive.[23]

In industrial society, the major resource is cheap, plentiful energy—water power and fossil fuels. The main occupational mode is the fabrication of goods—manufacture, machinery, factories. The technology grown out of science and invention, yielding new machines for mass production and requiring large sums of capital to initiate the manufacturing process. Here the design is to improve on nature, to take natural raw materials and turn them into new products: steel, textiles, automobiles, airplanes, appliances; or to create new materials, such as nylon, dacron, polyester, and plastic. Efficiency is the goal to be achieved through technical means—by rationalizing the production process (i.e., specialization of function) and the work of the labor force (i.e., division of labor).[24]

With the transition to postindustrial society comes a reliance on information as the major resource base. Information technologies emerge alongside industrial machine technologies; research and development become as important as production. The new technologies are designed to process information, first mechanically and then electronically. The symbol of postindustrial society is the electronic computer, whose applications impinge on every aspect of personal and social life. The computer stores, retrieves, and manipulates facts and data. It's the ultimate tool for the ultimate resource—the human being. Programs (knowledge) run computers. The design is one of person-to-person and person-to-computer. Education and the production of knowledge are the paramount industries.[25]

Another way of comparing the three forms of society is by analyzing the types of occupations that predominate in each societal form. In preindustrial societies the primary occupations are the dominant ones: agriculture, fishing, and mining. In industrial societies, there is still a need for a part of the labor force to be engaged in primary occupations, but the majority of workers participate in secondary occupations such as manufacturing, construction, transportation, and engineering. Also in industrial societies the tertiary occupation come into existence: utilities, banking and commerce, insurance, and education. As the transition to postindustrial society occurs, the quaternary occupations appear, and they, combined with the tertiary type, tend to dominate, although here too some of the workforce still practices primary and secondary occupations. At this stage, as few as four percent of the labor force is engaged in agriculture.

Throughout most of 1982 and 1983, John Naisbitt's *Megatrends* was a major national bestseller. In his book he pointed to ten new "from/to" directions in American society.[26] These are listed in Table 4.

Table 4
Naisbitt's New Directions[27]

From	------>	To
1. Industrial society		Information society
2. Forced technology		High tech/high touch
3. National economy		World economy
4. Short term		Long term
5. Centralization		Decentralization
6. Institutional help		Self-help
7. Representative democracy		Participatory democracy
8. Hierarchies		Networking
9. North		South
10. Either/Or		Multiple option

Naisbitt claims that "caught between eras, we experience turbulence. Yet, amid the sometimes painful and uncertain present, the restructuring of America proceeds unrelentingly."[28] What are the interpretations of the ten new structurings?

Direction #1. The United States has made the shift from industrial to postindustrial society, which Naisbitt calls the "information society: an economy based on the creation and distribution of information."[29]

Direction #2. "High tech/high touch is a formula—to describe the way we have responded to technology....Whenever new technology is introduced into society, there must be a counterbalancing human response—that is, *high touch*—or the technology is rejected."[30] The high tech of the intensive care units in hospitals is counterbalanced by the hospice movement and the concern for the quality of death.[31]

Direction #3. Interdependence of national economies has been on the increase since 1945. "No longer do we have the luxury of operating within an isolated, self-sufficient, national economic system...."[32]

Direction #4. Corporations under pressure from boards of directors and stockholders, and government officials under pressure from periodic elections, pursue short-term goals. American leaders, however, are learning from Japan and other nations the value of long-term, cooperatively developed economic plans.[33]

Direction #5. Disenchanted with federal government initiatives to solve social problems and with large, bureaucratic, impersonal corporations and institutions, Americans are feeling greater efficacy and success with grassroots efforts at state and local levels and at the plant and work group levels in industry.[34]

Direction #6. Faith in government, schools, hospitals, and businesses is on the wane, and people are relying more on self and friends than on established institutions. Examples of this are food cooperatives, women's networks, holistic health, home schooling, and people's clinics.[35]

Direction #7. In an era of instantaneous communication via the electronic media, representative government has become cumbersome and inconvenient. A new "ethic of participation is spreading bottom up across America and radically altering the way we think people in institutions should be governed. Citizens, workers, and consumers are demanding and getting a greater voice in government, business, and the market place."[36]

Direction #8. Government and industry are organized in top-down hierarchies. "The failure of hierarchies to solve society's problems forced people to talk to one another—and that was the beginning of networks."[37] These are informal clusters of persons with similar interests, who are held together by conferences, phone calls, books (common readings), travel, newsletters, workshops, grapevines, coalitions, radio, computers, and audio/video tapes.[38]

Direction #9. "More Americans are living in the South and West, leaving behind the old industrial cities of the North."[39] In the 1980 census, "for the first time in American history the South and West had more people than the North and East."[40] The shift of population reflects the same shift of wealth and economic activity.[41]

Direction #10. "From a narrow either/or society with a limited range of personal choices, we are exploding into a free-wheeling, multiple-option society."[42] "In a relatively sort time, the unified mass society has fractionalized into many diverse groups of people with a wide array of differing tastes and values, what advertisers call a market-segmented, market-decentralized society."[43]

Transformationist. The last of our trio of futures perspectives is that of the transformationist. On the continuum from continuity to change, the transformationist stands near the extreme change end. Here is a futurist who views past and future history as a series of discontinuities, of disjunctions and revolutions, all involving crisis, disorientation, and trauma. This chronicler of revolutions sees that dissatisfaction and disaffection must reach near-universal proportions before a cataclysmic change, which shakes the foundations (culture and values) of a society, can occur.

Like the transitionist, the transformationist also talks about shifts *from* one condition *to* a different one. The difference between the two positions lies in the speed and extent of change. Whereas the transitionist expects change over a period of centuries, the transformationist looks for the dramatic dislocations that happen in a few years or decades, even though the seeds of revolution had been incubating for a much longer time. While the transitionist anticipates significant changes within a society, he/she doesn't expect the entire infrastructure, the culture, ideology and values, of the society to be eroded and replaced. The transformationist does expect such deep-rooted and far-reaching changes — a true revolution.

In oversimplified terms, the transformationist believes that things have to get worse before they get better. The society is healthy and prosperous for a time; then contradictions surface that lead to a complex of unsolved problems; a crisis occurs, alerting the members of the society to its flaws; crisis upon crisis occur in quick succession, bringing on revolution. But when the clues to the fatal flaws first appear, a significant minority of societal members, as individuals or in groups, begin to innovate, invent, and experiment, creating the potential building blocks for a new society. With the revolution also comes the rudimentary structures of the new society. These structures are the new means for personal and social fulfillment in the new society.

As futurist, the transformationist looks for two types of indicators: (1) sources of contradiction, alienation, and potential crises, and (2) types of personal and social experiments that have the potential to overcome the flaws in the present social fabric. For example, indicators of contradiction and possible breakdown include critical excesses of poverty, crime, racism, sexism, pollution, inflation, unemployment, substance abuse, child abuse, famine and hunger, nuclear threat, overdevelopment, and overconsumption.

In another vein, one can point to the malaise created by three historical disconnections: (1) of humans from nature, (2) of person from person, and (3) of self (outer) from self (inner). Or one could observe the failures of Western industrialized societies to provide: (1) opportunities for feeling efficacious, (2) equitable distribution of wealth and power, (3) responsible management of new technologies, (4) compelling visions of desirable futures, and (5) balance between material and spiritual needs.

Examples of the second type of indicator — new, potentially promising personal and social experiments — might include these recent developments or movements:

1. Advocacy of appropriate or intermediate technology (as opposed to "high tech").

2. "Small Is Beautiful" movement (as expounded by the late E. F. Schumacher).

3. Self-restraint (in buying) and self-reliance (in fixing and creating).

4. Voluntary simplicity movement.

5. Intentional, experimental communities (e.g., Arcosanti in Arizona and Findhorn in Scotland).

6. Reruralization movement (from center to periphery).

7. Study of paranormal phenomena (e.g., telepathy, remote viewing, pre-cognition, telekinesis, thought photography, and involuntary processes).

8. The study and practice of psychotechnologies: psychotherapy, meditation techniques (e.g., TM and yoga), est, Testalt therapy, biofeedback, logotherapy, and dream analysis.

Two transformationist futurists are Theodore Roszak (*The Making of a Counter Culture*, 1969; *Where the Wasteland Ends*, 1972; *Unfinished Animal*, 1975; *Person/Planet*, 1978) and Willis W. Harman (*An Incomplete Guide to the Future*, 1976).

Since the 1960s, Theodore Roszak has been an outspoken, articulate critic of American establishment, mainstream society, and at the same time has been a spokesman for countercultural groups and movements. As the cover of one of his books illustrates—by use of a mirror—each of us is an "Unfinished Animal," a member of a species that is continuously evolving.[44] He has faith that what is emerging is "an Aquarian Age filled with wonders and well-being, a transformation of human personality...which is of evolutionary proportions, a shift of consciousness fully as epoch-making as the appearance of speech or of the tool-making talents in our cultural repertory."[45] What is bringing on this evolutionary transformation are "the new ecological awareness...with its sense of allegiance to the planet as a whole,...[and] the rapid convergence of age-old spiritual disciplines and contemporary psychotherapy...."[46]

On the "Aquarian Frontier" Roszak sees twelve major "points of entry." These are:[47]

1. Judeo-Christian Revivals—e.g., new pentecostalism, charismatic congregations, Jewish Havurot movement.

2. Eastern Religions—e.g., Zen and Tibetan Buddhism, Taoism, Yoga, Sufism.

3. Esoteric Studies—e.g., comparative religion, theosophy, anthroposophy, Kabbalism (Jewish).

4. Eupsychian Therapies—e.g., Jungian psychiatry, psychosynthesis, Arica, transpersonal psychology.

5. Etherealized Healing—e.g., integral healing, homeopathy, acupuncture, hypnotherapy.

6. Body Therapies—e.g., Rolfing, bioenergetics, massage, aikido, sensory awareness.

7. Neo-Primitivism and Paganism—e.g., philosophical mythology, sorcery, shamanism, voluntary primitive lifestyles.

8. Organicism—e.g., ecological mysticism, macrobiotics, natural foods cults, biorhythms.

9. Wild Science—e.g., altered states of consciousness, ESP, split-brain research, synergistics.

10. Psychics, Spiritualists, Occult Groups—e.g., Edgar Cayce, Eckankar, Stele Group.

11. Psychotronics—e.g., neural cybernetics, media mysticism, mind-altering drugs.

12. Pop Culture—e.g., science fiction, metaphysical fantasy, acid rock, laser light shows.

Roszak summarizes the import of this potpourri:

> But perhaps the most wisely appealing quality of the Aquarian sign is the hope it offers as water-bearer to a parched and dying culture. Aquarius, the bringer of water, an emblem of life in the midst of a wasteland. Or such is the promise of the frontier before us, though we must bear in mind that, where fertility is not matched by careful cultivation, it yields no livable human habitat, but instead the deadly luxuriance of swamp or jungle.[48]

This is the cry of the transformationist: Transform or die! And if transformation is chosen, expect "the traumas of rebirth."[49]

In a later book, Roszak transcends national frontiers by linking the transformation of the individual to the fate of the planet. *Person/Planet* continues the theme of "creative disintegration," of the new emerging from the ashes of the old. But not only in one or a few societies, for "the needs of the planet and the needs of the person have become one...."[50] "At the same time that our sense of personality deepens, our sense of ecological responsibility increases. Just as we grow more acutely concerned for the sanctity of the person, so we grow more anxious for the well-being of the planetary environment."[51]

Finding a "personal scale of life" means focusing on environments where one can act and make a difference. These contexts are home, school, work, and the city. Comfort and concern in these milieus prepare one to accept the world's diversity and to act as steward of the planet's ecosystem.[52]

From his bases in the San Francisco area—Stanford University, SRI International, and the Institute for Noetic Sciences—Willis Harman combines an academic background in physics, engineering, and economics with an experiential background in the human potential movement and the study of ways of knowing and social policy futures. He ranges broadly across fields of knowledge but avoids superficiality and oversimplification.

In his one slender volume on social futures, Harman first argues that "the industrial-era paradigm" is flawed and too limiting. Next, he analyzes four industrial-era dilemmas (i.e., growth, work-roles, world distribution, and control). Finally, he presents a new image of humanity, a scenario of "the transindustrial era," and a set of change strategies.[53]

The industrial era, Harman asserts, suffers from its successes and excesses. For example, the health sciences have succeeded in reducing infant mortality, which has led to burgeoning populations. Such "problems of technological success" keep increasing and then tend to interact in complexes creating a crisis of crises.[54]

One of these success/problem paradoxes is "the growth dilemma." In this case, the industrialized world has enjoyed the benefits of plentiful consumer goods, but growth at the levels of the period, 1945-1975, cannot be sustained due to the new scarcities of fossil fuels, minerals, water, arable land, and the capacity of environments to absorb wastes. Yet, "the industrialized countries of the world are structured in such a way that their economics demand growth...."[55]

A second problem is "the work-roles dilemma," which is the reverse side of the growth dilemma. "If...economic growth slows down for any reason, a whole group of work-related problems will be exacerbated, including unemployment and the threat of unemployment, the economic and social costs of vast welfare systems, poverty and malnutrition and affluence, widespread underemployment and attendant work dissatisfaction, and discontent among the young [kept out of the economy] and the aging [pushed out]."[56]

A third paradox is "the world distribution dilemma":

> We cannot risk the international instability that results from the vast disparities between the rich and poor nations, yet neither of the obvious solutions—making the poor nations richer or the rich nations poorer—seems feasible. The world probably cannot afford to have the gap closed through making the poor nations as productive, consuming, and polluting as the rich nations; at the same time, the rich nations are not likely to choose voluntarily to become less materialistic and more frugal.[57]

The fourth dilemma concerns who is in the saddle: technology or humanity? "How can we exercise needed societal control over technology without sacrificing individual liberty?"[58] To gain control over technological development and use, will we lose the fundamentals of free enterprise and democracy?

Dealing with the dilemmas, argues Harman, requires an alternative to "the industrial-era paradigm"—not modification but a new paradigm. The new paradigm will be rooted in new conceptions of human nature.

2. HUMAN FUTURES

There are numerous ways to map the territory of the future—from statistical extrapolation to imaginative science fiction, from demography to poetry, from architectural forms to synthesized music. Topics of interest to futurists are wide ranging and almost unlimited in number. Four domains, however, receive considerable attention from many futurists who reflect a broad, general perspective in their forecasts. These domains are: (1) emerging values (at the personal, community, and societal levels), (2) frontiers of knowledge (in current academic disciplines and in the "slippery realms" of consciousness and paranormal phenomena), (3) technological developments (in weapons systems, in medicine and pharmacology, and in genetic engineering), and (4) persistent social issues (such as energy source depletion, hunger, poverty, pollution). Trends and forecasts will be examined in each of these four domains.

The Domain of Values

"The unity of a culture consists in the fact that all valuations are mutually shared in some degree."[59] A system of values, an ideology, is the infrastructure that supports and gives coherence to all of a society's institutions. In each society this values/ideology base is relatively stable, though at crucial times it enters a state of flux when new emergent values challenge traditional values. At such times, the resulting conflict and strife within a society usually lead to a modification or new synthesis of the values/ideology base, or to an almost totally new infrastructure and, therefore, to a new society born of revolution.

It is highly likely that in the modern world social values are in constant turmoil, either bubbling just beneath the surface of daily events or boiling over in the debates over ubiquitous social issues. Constant tension seems to exist in every society between traditional values and emerging values, creating perturbations in the infrastructure that normally result in the evolvement of a new set of values. Clearly, such is the case in the United States today.

The American republic was born of revolution, yet its ideology was an importation from the shores of Western Europe and the islands of Great Britain. American values derived from five related (and on occasion contradictory) traditions: (1) the Protestant ethic, (2) the Puritan temper, (3) bourgeois capitalism, (4) republican democracy, and (5) Western philosophy. Like one of the five-pointed stars in the flag of the new American nation, these five value clusters were merged into a new ideology.

At the heart of the American ideology are the Protestant ethic and the Puritan temper, two "codes that emphasized work, sobriety, frugality, sexual restraint, and a forbidding attitude toward life. They defined the nature of moral conduct and social respectability."[60] They were combined in "the man of action, who was also the man of God."[61] Separately, their exemplars were Benjamin Franklin, the man of action, "the pragmatic and utilitarian Protestant," and Jonathan Edwards, the man of God, "the aethetic and intuitive Puritan."[62] In these two eighteenth-century figures we have "the essence of the American character: the piety and torment of Jonathan Edwards, obsessed with human depravity, and the practicality and expedience of Benjamin Franklin, oriented to a world of possibility and gain."[63]

The complementary concepts of the Puritan temper and the Protestant ethic contributed to what Gunnar Myrdal has called "the American Creed"—the values of self-denial or endurance of distress; deferred gratification; sexual restraint and chastity; frugality and thrift; industriousness; self-control, temperance, and moderation; order and punctuality; humility and charity; and the survival of the fittest as derived from the Calvinist idea of predestination or "the elect of God."

As Max Weber argued so persuasively and eloquently, there is an intimate relationship between the Protestant ethic and the practice of bourgeois capitalism. The values in each tradition are mutually supportive: the successful entrepreneur is easily justified and confirmed by appeal to such values as resolution, frugality, industry, order, punctuality, striving, and especially to the concept of "the elect of God" who might be viewed as preordained to "success."[64]

The values inherent in bourgeois capitalism are the profit motive, competitiveness, scarcity as a function of unlimited demand with limited supply, a free market economy, contrived demand through advertising and "forced" obsolescence, social class distinctions based on wealth and possessions, materialism, acquisitiveness, conspicuous consumption, meritocratic hiring and promotion, and the priority of private property ownership rights.

In addition to Protestant, Puritan, and capitalistic values, the American Creed also comprises democratic value orientations. These are enhancement of human dignity, rational consent of the governed, rule of the majority, guarantees of individual and minority rights and of due process, the quality of freedom or liberty or independence, and the search for equality and equity in conjoint living.

Finally, the ideology of United States society contains a number of values that have pervaded the development of Western civilization and are embedded in Western philosophy and science. These value positions are rationality, empiricism and experimentation, humanism, dualistic analysis, and various forms of reductionism, especially the quantification of phenomena.

The American Creed, then, is a composite ideology that gradually coalesced during the seventeenth/eighteenth centuries and has endured with some modification for the past 200 years. Even though the structure of American society has changed in the past two centuries, the ideological infrastructure has remained intact:

> It is in the character of ideologies not only to reflect or justify an underlying reality but,
> once launched, to take on a life of their own...Thus an ideology gnawed at, worried to
> the bone, argued about, dissected, and restated by an army of essayists, moralists,
> and intellectuals becomes a force in its own right.[65]

An ideology is most apt to be questioned during times of social trauma and strife, during what are commonly called "hard times" or when the society is engaged in war. Thus, in America, changes in social values and in the conditions of social living occurred for the most part in conjunction with wars and economic crises, but also over longer stretches of time in response to powerful though slowly evolving trends. Events and developments in the history of the United States that had the greatest impact in changing social values and structures were the Civil War, World War I, the Great Depression, World War II, the Vietnam War, urbanization, industrialization, and the civil rights movement, as well as selected technologies such as the steam engine and railroads, the factory system, the internal combustion engine and automobiles, the airplane and rocketry, and electronic communications (radio, television, and computers).

The pollster, Daniel Yankelovich, sees much the same situation for the past decade. In his recent volume, *New Rules*, the subtitle conveys the message: *Searching for Self-fulfillment in a World Turned Upside Down*. He explains that his book "concerns a particular expression of American culture—the search for 'self-fulfillment' and the predicaments it creates for the individual and the nation." These seekers try life experiments that "often collide violently with traditional rules, creating a national battle of moral norms." Thus, what we find in American society in the 1980s are the conflicts and contradictions between traditional norms and values and those of the seekers.[66]

Yankelovich found in his polls (and in polls of others also) that some traditional norms still command overwhelming assent. These state that people:[67]

1. Would still have children if they had to do it over again (90 percent).

2. Feel use of hard drugs is morally wrong (87 percent).

3. Feel it's up to parents to educate teenagers about birth control (84 percent).

4. Feel mate-swapping is morally wrong (81 percent).

16

5. Disapprove of married women having affairs (79 percent).

6. Disapprove of married men having affairs (76 percent).

7. Agree that a woman should put her husband and children ahead of her career (77 percent).

8. Want their children to be better off and more successful than they are (74 percent).

On the other hand, there are also "major changes in the norms guiding American life." Some of these are:[68]

1. Whereas over 70 percent of respondents in 1938 "disapproved of a married woman earning money if she has a husband capable of supporting her," by 1978 this was down to about 25 percent.

2. No longer is a family with four or more children considered ideal (1945); in 1980 the ideal is two children.

3. In 1957, a woman who remained unmarried must have been sick, neurotic, or immoral (80 percent); but by 1978 the percent had decreased to 25 percent.

4. In 1937, only 25 percent of those polled would vote for a qualified woman nominee for president, but by 1980 the percent was almost 80.

5. About 85 percent of subjects in 1967 condemned premarital sex as morally wrong, whereas in 1979 it was less than 40 percent.

6. In 1979, 75 percent agreed that it was morally acceptable to be single and have children.

7. Over 60 percent approved of interracial marriages in 1977.

8. About 75 percent of working women in 1976 would go on working even if they didn't have to.

In considering the goals of the self-fulfillment seekers, Yankelovich notes three dilemmas they face, what he calls their "triple bind." First, they have a tremendous range of choices available to them, but they don't know how to make appropriate ones. "The question of what to commit to and sacrifice for thus remains forever open, making their lives unsettled." Second, "their goals take for granted continued affluence, abundant career opportunities, flexible work arrangements, low-cost travel, diverse outlets for personal creativity, low burdens of responsibility," while the political and economic scenes in the 1980s become less and less hospitable to these attitudes. Third, their concern for self-fulfillment is an inner quest, which works fine during stable, peaceful times, but which is almost useless in times of personal crisis.[69]

Yankelovich further observes that "perhaps the sharpest shift in American attitudes has been a steady erosion of trust in government and other institutions, falling from a peak of trust and confidence in the late fifties to a trough of mistrust in the early eighties."[70] For example, he reports the following survey research findings from a University of Michigan study in which "the changes move only in one direction—from trust to mistrust":[71]

1. "The people running the government in Washington are smart people who know what they are doing"—from 69 percent to 29 percent.

2. "You can trust the government to do what is right most or all of the time"—from 56 percent to 29 percent.

3. "The government is run for the benefit of all, rather than for a few big interests"—from 72 percent to 35 percent.

4. "Public officials care what people like me think" — from 71 percent to 33 percent.

5. "The government wastes a lot of the money we pay in taxes" — from 42 percent to 77 percent.

What has happened in the past two or three decades? Yankelovich believes that "doubts have now set in, and Americans now believe that the old giving/getting compact needlessly restricts the individual while advancing the power of large institutions — government and business particularly — who use the power to enhance their own interests at the expense of the public."[72]

As self-fulfillment begins to replace the ethic of self-denial, however, a void is created in the social realm. Excessive self-indulgence destroys all commitment to community, leaving no social ethic. "Any viable social ethic has real work to do: it binds the individual to the society; it synchronizes society's goals with those of each person; it holds society together and keeps it from degenerating into a chaos of competing interests."[73] Yankelovich thinks a new ethic is emerging in embryonic form out of "two kinds of commitments: closer and deeper personal relationships, and the switch from certain instrumental values to sacred/expressive ones."[74]

At SRI International in Menlo Park, California, a fascinating survey research project was carried out by the staff of the "Values and Lifestyles Program" under the direction of Arnold Mitchell. The findings of the project were reported in 1983 in the book, *The Nine American Lifestyles*.[75] "The survey asked over 800 specific questions on a great range of topics. Sample size exceeded 1,600."[76] Out of this extensive research came the Values and Lifestyle (VALS) typology, summarized in Table 5.

Table 5
VALS Typology[77]

	Percent of Adult Population	
A. Need-Driven Groups	11%	
1. Survivors		4%
2. Sustainers		7%
B. Outer-Directed Groups	67%	
3. Belongers		35%
4. Emulators		10%
5. Achievers		22%
C. The Inner-Directed Groups	20%	
6. I-AM-ME		5%
7. Experiential		7%
8. Societally Conscious		8%
D. The Combined Outer- and Inner-Directed Group	2%	
9. Integrated		2%
	————	————
	100%	100%

1. **Survivors**—These are the old, intensely poor, fearful, far removed from the cultural mainstream.

2. **Sustainers**—They are angry, resentful, street-wise, living on the edge of poverty, and involved in the underground economy.

3. **Belongers**—This category includes aging, conventional, content, intensely patriotic, traditional, middle Americans.

4. **Emulators**—This group comprises young, ambitious, flashy persons who are trying to break into the system.

5. **Achievers**—These are middle-aged, prosperous, self-assured leaders and builders of the American dream.

6. **I-AM-ME**—They are very young, narcissistic, impulsive, exhibitionists who are in a transitional state to inner direction.

7. **Experiential**—This category comprises youthful, artistic seekers of direct experiences who are intensely oriented toward inner growth.

8. **Societally Conscious**—These are mission-oriented, mature, successful persons who are out to change the world.

9. **Integrated**—This group is psychologically mature, tolerant, flexible, understanding, and able to see "the big picture."

As values and attitudes underlie these nine lifestyles, it is clear that American society may be best characterized as one exemplifying *diversity*. Within this loosely cohering nation are many diverse personal preferences: family patterns; political, economic, and societal goals; religious/spiritual beliefs; and educational goals.

The author of *The Nine American Lifestyles* identifies a cyclic scheme for how the values base of a society changes. He calls the process the "Values Rhythms of a Society," in which root values pass through a cycle of seasons (see Figure 4). In this cycle, the place to begin is in *Autumn*, when a partic-

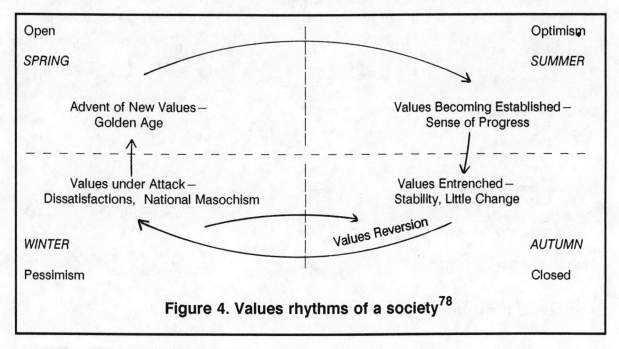

Figure 4. Values rhythms of a society[78]

ular set of traditional values has been entrenched for a while, and when there is relative stability in societal institutions. In the United States, this "season" might be equated to the period 1918-1927 (from just after World War I to immediately before the Great Depression) or to the 1950s. Next comes *Winter*, a time of crisis, confusion, even revolution, when the traditional values of *Autumn* are challenged. It is at this time also that reactionary forces attempt to return the society to the calmer days of a recent or even distant past—"Values Reversion." *Winter* might be exemplified by the New Deal era (also the Great Depression), as old and new values clashed, or by the 1960s followed by the nostalgia of the 1970s. Notice that each sector of the diagram, in addition to having a seasonal label, is depicted as (starting with *Autumn*) "Closed," "Pessimism," "Open," and "Optimism." "Closed" in *Autumn* means that the society is not receptive to new ideas or values during this period. "Pessimism" in *Winter* suggests the society is confused and self-critical (Dissatisfactions, National Masochism) in this era. Isn't *Spring* always "Open" to all that is new—the blooming of values, the Golden Age? *Summer* is "Optimism," the stage of contentment as new values become institutionalized and euphoria reigns.

Mitchell's cycle of "Values Rhythms" implies that, as in most arenas of human personal and social life, crisis precedes change. If today we in Western societies are somewhere in *Winter*, perhaps nearer to the advent of *Spring*, then during the last half of the 1980s and into the 1990s we can expect some values shifts and accompanying lifestyle changes. Mitchell forecasts such shifts and changes in the VALS Typology, as can be seen in Table 6.

In this table, several significant projected changes, both increases and decreases, should be noted. First, virtually all the change occurs in the Outer-Directed, Inner-Directed, and Integrated (Combined) categories. Second, the major decrease in percent is for the Outer-Directed, specifically Belongers. Growth occurs mainly with the Inner-Directed, Societally Conscious, and doubles for the Integrated.

Table 6
Renaissance Future: Estimates of Lifestyle Shifts
Between 1980 and 1990[79]

	1980 Percent	1980 Number (Millions)	1990 Percent	1990 Number (Millions)
Need-Driven Groups	11	17	10	18
Survivors	4	6	4	7
Sustainers	7	11	6	11
Outer-Directed Groups	67	108	60	108
Belongers	35	57	30	54
Emulators	10	16	10	18
Achievers	22	35	20	36
Inner-Directed Groups	20	32	26	47
I-AM-ME	5	8	4	7
Experiential	7	11	9	16
Societally Conscious	8	13	13	24
Integrated Group	2	3	4	7

Number aged 18 and over.

20

If out of crisis comes change, then a crucial question is: Are we presently in the midst of a crisis? Many futurists, though by no means a majority, argue that we are not only in a crisis, but in a Crisis of Crises or Megacrisis:

> Though no one can know what future historians will call our period of history, we may provisionally term it the Era of the Megacrisis because it is far more than a crisis by the standards of the past; it is a supercrisis.[80]

This quotation seems to imply that there exist concurrent crises, complexly interrelated. Edward Cornish, founder and president of the World Future Society, goes on to offer this list of current crises:[81]

1. Lack of control of population growth.

2. War, violence, and the growth and threat of totalitarianism.

3. Planetary impoverishment of resources, famine, and starvation.

4. Miscellaneous possible horrors: "insane" nations, nuclear crime, economic collapse, death of oceans, climate extremes, destruction of the ozone layer, racial strife, family breakdown, worldwide unemployment and underemployment, loss of religious belief.

In dealing with values shifts, a common practice is to present value rubrics in two parallel columns, with the list on the left referring to *traditional* values, those from which *emergent* values, the list on the right, are shifting away. The list on the left may be titled "Traditional" or merely "From," while the parallel list on the right may be headed "Emergent" or "To." Table 7 represents the author's view of current value shifts in American society.

The Domain of Knowledge

As a species, humans learn from their own experiences as well as from those of generations that preceded them. Human beings both preserve and create knowledge. Further, our knowledge growth occurs both by normal accretion and, on occasion, by revolutionary leaps or shifts.

"In our time," says Soviet physicist Arkadii Migdal, "the frontiers of the possible have been pushed back so far that they merge into those of wonderland."[82] For physicists and astronomers, the universe has become more mind than material, more idea than matter, more filled with paradox than with certainty. Mysterious, strange wonders abound: quasars, pulsars, and black holes; backwards time, antimatter, and negative mass. We are insatiably curious—leaving footprints on the Moon and a "dead" robot on Mars. We beam messages from a radio telescope at Arecibo, Puerto Rico, toward this and that distant star, always in search of a neighbor, a soulmate, a friend in the universe. What will we find? What will we learn today, tomorrow, next year? What will emerge from Pandora's Box by the year 2000?

We can conclude from the history of our species that knowledge is continually incomplete, yet almost always sufficient for the survival of a people at a particular time and place. We constantly seek to alter and extend the frontiers of knowledge in every realm, but each society "chooses" a select set of realms in which to concentrate creative efforts. Thus, in ancient Egypt the clergy and aristocracy created knowledge primarily in the realms of architecture, agriculture (especially in irrigation), military science, and religion; while in the United States during the nineteenth century the growth of industrialization was accompanied by spurts of new knowledge in the realms of physics, chemistry, metallurgy, and engineering. The flow of knowledge production is generally in those directions most compatible with a society's images of the future.

Probably the most productive mode for creating knowledge in the past four or five centuries has been science. By "science" is meant the methods employed rather than the scientific disciplines involved (e.g., physics). Science-as-method is a set of assumptions and procedures for describing and

Table 7
Values Shifts[83]

From (Traditional Values)	**To** (Emergent Values)
1. Self-denial, endurance of stress, and deferred gratification	1. Pursuit of immediate pleasures or hedonism
2. Sexual taboos and constraints	2. Sexual permissiveness or openness
3. Self-control, belief that hard work yields success, striving to achieve	3. Self-actualization and self-expressiveness, acceptance and expression of feelings, self-realization
4. "Survival of the fittest"	4. "Survival of the wisest," the individual's survival entwined with species, global survival
5. Progress equated with growth, promotion of increased consumption and number of consumers	5. Limits to growth, search for ecological balances, stress on qualitative aspects of progress
6. Competitiveness—a win-lose, either-or attitude	6. Cooperation, conflict resolution and reduction, win-win attitude
7. Materialism, acquisitiveness, and conspicuous consumption	7. Focus on essentials, greater desire for quality and durability of goods
8. Social class distinction based primarily on wealth	8. Greater concern for equality and equity, class distinctions based on multiple criteria (de-emphasis on accumulated wealth), which will tend to blur class lines
9. Preoccupation with private property ownership rights	9. Increasing pressures to insure basic human rights—nationally and globally, greater concern for "the commons" that are shared collectively (e.g., water, parks, air, neighborhoods)
10. Government by isolated elected officials in state and national capitals	10. Government by association, involvement, and participation of the entire citizenry; increased pressures from interest groups
11. Nationalism, exclusive national sovereignties as loci of loyalties, independence of nation-states	11. World order models, transnational economic grouping as bases for regional political grouping (e.g., European Common Market), regional and world federalisms, interdependence of nations
12. Freedom or liberty or independence, individualism	12. Mutuality of concern, cooperative processes, greater attention to interpersonal relations and quality of conjoint living
13. Nationalism, empiricism, scientism, dualistic analysis, reductionism, and quantification	13. Renewed reliance on faith and feeling, practice of meditative modes, global humanism, blending of Taoist and Buddhist world views with those of Judeo-Christian tradition, abandoning the search for value-free knowledge, greater trust in all human ways of knowing

explaining phenomena. These usually include both inductive and deductive logic, empiricism and experimentalism, a belief in an *orderly* physical universe that can be directly comprehended in a rational manner, objective control of all variables, public and replicable procedures and conclusions, and a faith that the objective world is essentially separate from and independent of the subjective experience of the researcher.

Faith in science as *the* path to reliable and comprehensive knowledge is typically justified by pointing to one or more of the following aspects of science: (1) its simple yet elegant explanations of physical phenomena; (2) the ingenuity of its heroes: Copernicus, Galileo, Kepler, Newton, Maxwell, Einstein, Watson and Crick, and perhaps a hundred others; (3) its cumulative growth from one historical synthesis to the next; and (4) its use as a springboard to invention and technology.

In the past few decades, a number of philosophers and a few scientists have questioned one or more of the premises upon which the scientific enterprise has been constructed. Some of the critics challenge the supremacy of science as *the* mode of knowing about reality, while others castigate scientists for their seeming lack of concern for values, especially in regard to social issues. Still others point to what they consider to be outmoded assumptions of science such as: (1) Reason is *the* supreme tool in discovering new knowledge! (2) The universe is inherently orderly and physical! or (3) The only reliable truth is that which is empirically verifiable![84]

In the realm of knowledge, the future holds prospects for new knowledge derived via the current paradigms in science; the probable emergence of new paradigms and new disciplines that incorporate subjective experience, value dimensions, and the neglected phenomena of paranormal or psychic human behaviors; the development of new modes of knowledge creation, especially in the field of futures forecasting; and a new generation of technological inventions.

Of the 100 or so disciplines of knowledge, it is difficult to detect in which ones major significant breakthroughs will occur. Some clues do exist, however, as to where discoveries may take place. For example, in the natural sciences the momentum seems to have shifted from physics to biology, especially biochemistry, where investigations in brain research and in recombinant DNA research seem to be most promising. Kenneth Clark asserts:

> We might be on the threshold of that type of scientific, biochemical intervention [into the brain] which could stabilize and make dominant the moral and ethical propensities of man and subordinate, if not eliminate, his negative and primitive tendencies.[85]

Thus, we may have the biochemistry and pharmacology of peace.

Recombinant DNA research is currently quite controversial due to its inherent danger of creating possibly lethal new organisms by accident, such as a new virus that the human body is unable to combat. Nevertheless, with appropriate safeguards, this type of research holds potential for the production of new organisms to attack diseases in both humans and plants, as well as means to eliminate many genetic defects.

Then there is the recent interest in split-brain research—in the biopsychology of the left and right hemispheres of the brain. At this time we can tentatively conclude that the left hemisphere controls "analytic and reductionist" thinking while the right side emphasizes "more holistic and integrative" thought.[86]

In the past decade, interest has increased in the field of consciousness research—the study of altered states of subjective awareness and of extrasensory perceptions and skills. Curiously, many investigators have come to this area from backgrounds in the natural sciences, especially physics. As Jacob Bronowski put it: "Knowledge is our destiny. Self-knowledge, at last bringing together the experience of the arts and the explanations of science, waits ahead of us."[87]

The great frontier of future knowledge is the study of the person—of mind, body, and spirit:

> Among the most fundamental challenges to present belief systems is the concept that consciousness is primary to matter.... From an Eastern perspective the dynamics of consciousness are the forces governing the behavior of matter.[88]

As the Nobel laureate in physics, Werner Heisenberg, so aptly stated:

> It seems...that developments in many fields of science and technology are running in the same direction: away from the immediate sensory present into an, at first, uncanny emptiness and distance, whence the great connections of the world become discernible.[89]

There is an intimate and profound link to be found between the inner space of the individual and the outer space of the stars.

Thomas Kuhn, noted historian of scientific revolutions, informs us that the growth of knowledge occurs in cycles. A complete cycle describes a scientific revolution, what Kuhn calls a "paradigm shift," and comprises six steps:[90]

1. At the outset, the practitioners in a particular scientific discipline, say chemistry, work on the *old paradigm*, a set of theoretical constructions that guide current research. Since this step generally extends over a longer time period than any of the succeeding ones, Kuhn refers to research activities during this period as "normal science."

2. Gradually, however, *anomalies* crop up that can't be accounted for with the old paradigm. As anomalous phenomena and results accumulate, existing theories become suspect and insufficient as a paradigm for further research.

3. At this point, the discipline enters a stage of *crisis*, as the old paradigm is no longer respected, yet no successor has been confirmed.

4. Next, one or more heroes appear on the scientific scene to propose a *new paradigm*; also vying for recognition are many would-be heroes. It is far from clear at this moment in history whose paradigm is the most viable.

5. A battle ensues as defenders of the old paradigm challenge, through heated debates, advocates of the several new paradigms. This is the stage of *revolutionary science*, when careers are made or destroyed, Nobel prizes won or lost, while the advance of knowledge hangs in the balance.

6. Many debates later, usually after pioneering experiments have confirmed the new theory, the *new paradigm is accepted* by the profession. Now, the new paradigm becomes the established paradigm, and then soon it is another old paradigm as normal science once again becomes the norm.

For each of the academic disciplines, over 100 in number, in which ones can we expect breakthroughs, or paradigm shifts, in the near future? It is virtually impossible to forecast such an event. One can conjecture that one or another discipline is ripe for the emergence of a new paradigm, but this merely suggests readiness. One can point, however, to certain clues and broad trends in the evolution of scientific knowledge. For example, in this century there has been a tendency to form new subjects from the conjunction of two older disciplines: biophysics, sociobiology, physical chemistry, social psychology, biochemistry, psychohistory. Further, one can point to both scientific and public interest in the space shuttle and planetary exploration, in brain research and the study of paranormal phenomena, and in the human potential of various psychotechnologies. Much media attention has been focused on genetics research and engineering, especially as they impinge on conflicting human values regarding birth and death. The research support funds that are easiest to obtain are those earmarked for the study of fatal and crippling diseases, thus assuring medical and pharmacological researchers of continuing interest in their fields.

Some physicists and a few psychologists think that new paradigms will emerge from the study of paranormal phenomena (i.e., Psi phenomena or extrasensory perception). In this realm two formidable problems are paramount: (1) determining if these types of events and phenomena do, in fact, occur or exist, and (2) if they are real, finding the psychophysical mechanisms that cause or bring about these peculiar manifestations. Those phenomena presently under study are telepathy, telekinesis, remote viewing, precognition, retrocognition, and various involuntary processes such as temperature, heartbeat, and breathing.

Willis Harman forecasts that by 1994 science will have adopted a whole new set of premises. The new science will be predicated on the following:[91]

1. Knowledge will be seen as inclusive rather than exclusive.

2. Science will be eclectic in methodology and in its definition of what constitutes knowledge. The controlled experiment will not be viewed as the only way to revealed truth.

3. The new knowledge paradigm will be hospitable to some sort of systematization of subjective experience, the domain that has heretofore largely been left to nonscience—the humanities and religion. Science will include the study of those experiences from which we derive our basic value commitments.

4. Science will foster open, participative inquiry in the sense of reducing the dichotomy between observer and observed, investigator and subject.

5. Science will be moral in the sense of investigating what values are wholesome for people (much in the sense that science of nutrition investigates that foods are wholesome for people), rather than a "value-free" inquiry.

6. Science will highlight a principle of complementarity, or reconciliation of such "opposites" as free will and determinism, materialism and transcendentalism, science and religion.

7. The new knowledge paradigm will incorporate some kind of concept of levels of consciousness, or levels of subjective experience, such that concepts and metaphors appropriate to one level do not necessarily fit another.

Perhaps the most significant potential development with respect to the future in the domain of knowledge is the emergence of "a knowledge society." The originator of this term, Robert Lane, describes the knowledge society as one in which, more than in other societies, its members:[92]

1. Inquire into the basis of their beliefs about people, nature, and society.

2. Are guided (perhaps unconsciously) by objective standards of veridical truth, and, at upper levels of education, follow scientific rules of evidence and inference in inquiry.

3. Devote considerable resources to this inquiry and thus have a large store of knowledge.

4. Collect, organize, and interpret their knowledge in a constant effort to extract meaning from it for the purposes at hand.

5. Employ this knowledge to illuminate (and perhaps modify) their values and goals as well as to advance them.

In a similar vein, Daniel Bell, the popularizer of the concept, "postindustrial society," considers the production and processing of information and knowledge to be a key characteristic of postindustrialism. For him, "intellectual technology" is the blending of research and development.[93]

John Platt describes the human creation of knowledge and technology as forms of "evolutionary jumps," similar in nature and effect as the stages in biological evolution. He produced the chart in Table 8 to illustrate his classification scheme.

Ever since Aristotle claimed that things in the world should be defined as either "A" or "Not A," Western societies have been plagued by the logic of dualisms. This "either-or" way of thinking or reasoning has presented us with such dichotomies as Mind-Body, Brain-Mind, Physical-Metaphysical, Body-Spirit, Emotional-Rational, Affective-Cognitive, Work-Play, Individual-Society, Theoretical-Practical, School-Society, and Teaching-Learning. In the past few decades, however, the confluence of two streams of thought challenges classical, dualistic logic. On the surface, these two modes of knowing seem uncongenial to each other, as one is a form of religious philosophy and the other a theory from the physical sciences. However unlikely, many scholars see remarkable similarities in perspective between Eastern religion (mainly Buddhism) and Western quantum physics. Gary Zukav asks: "Is it a coincidence that Buddhists exploring 'inner' reality a millennium ago and physicists exploring 'external' reality a millennium later both discovered that 'understanding' involves passing the barrier of paradox?"[94] The puzzle paradoxes of Zen (koans) and those of small particles/waves moving at the speed of light are similar in both form and solution. Fritjof Capra, in *The Tao of Physics*, invites the reader to compare two statements—one by the eminent quantum physicist, Niels Bohr and a second by the Indian mystic, Sri Aurobindo:[95]

> The great extension of our experience in recent years has brought to light the insufficiency of our simple mechanical conceptions and, as a consequence, has shaken the foundation on which the customary interpretation of observation was based.

> All things in fact begin to change their nature and appearance; one's whole experience of the world is radically different.... There is a new vast and deep way of experiencing, seeing, knowing, contacting things.

Just as the world of experience is seldom "this" or "that," so the world of the quantum theory is probabilistic in nature.

New knowledge will most certainly provide us with a clearer and more accurate view of both the world outside us and the world within us, but we must be prepared to acknowledge that seldom, if ever, again will we enjoy the certainty of the older science and logic. The knowledge of the future will require that we learn to live with and be comfortable with paradox and ambiguity, as well as with process and relativity.

The Domain of Technology

Every culture, every society has a technological base—a set of common tools and techniques. These may be as simple as a digging stick or a horse collar, or as complex as the space shuttle or bicameral government. Technology consists of the physical, material tool artifacts of a culture, but also includes processes (e.g., making steel) and organizational structures (e.g., corporation hierarchy). Technology is both machines and standardized processes, both "hardware" and "software."

In recent decades, Western industrialized high technology societies have become ambivalent, even jaded, with regard to new complex technological inventions. Some would say that the old cliche, "necessity is the mother of invention," has been replaced, through the use of forced obsolescence and unbridled advertising, by the reverse of this phrase, "invention is the mother of necessity." Even more serious is the claim that our kinds of technology tend to destroy the habitability of the planet. Although we enjoy our automobiles, we abhor their polluting effects; though our air conditioners make hot, dry climates livable, we deplore more and more dams for hydroelectric power and we fear nuclear generating plants; though we increase agricultural yields through the use of intense fertilization, we worry about nitrogen by-products and depletion of the soil; though we prize the possession of the products of industrial output, we lament the increasing costs of fossil fuels that drive these industries; we value precision and efficiency, but we find alienation and depersonalization intolerable. We are even beginning to suspect that further development of some technologies, especially weapons systems, may diminish our quality of life.

Nevertheless, we look to new technologies as messianic deliverers of better, benign aids to personal and societal fulfillment. Today the technologists, the inventors and tinkerers, are busy in their shops creating a vast new array of products for twenty-first century living. Hopefully our civilization will be around then to enjoy these new creations. Hopefully the new products will be life-enhancing rather than life-destroying.

Anticipated future technological developments, some just now becoming available and some on the drawing boards or barely discernible, can be grouped by categories for convenience of description. There are: (1) medical/health, (2) pharmacology, (3) agriculture, (4) automation/robots, (5) energy, (6) transportation, (7) space travel/colonies, and (8) communications (including technology-aided education). Unavoidably, there will be some overlap and redundancy.

Medical/Health

There are three general aspects to the improvement of healthful living: prenatal care and decisions (from the decision to have a child, through fertilization and fetus development, to birth and early postnatal care): lifelong preventive medicine, healthful living, and disease prevention; and extending life expectancy through the cure of fatal diseases and life-extension devices.

By the first decade of the twenty-first century, we can expect that the following will at least be available, if not in widespread use:

1. New prosthetic devices, such as fingers, hands, arms, feet, legs, will all be under the normal control of the patient's nervous system with some electronic assistance.

2. Laser canes are now available to the blind; the canes beep when an object or person is approaching.

3. Cryogenics will allow temporary suspension of life ("hibernation") in extremely low temperature environments.

4. Many hereditary and congenital defects and diseases will be eliminated, especially with the use of techniques of genetic engineering.

5. Cyborg techniques and inventions will make possible replacements or substitutes for human organs and senses.

6. Effective and convenient forms of appetite and weight control as well as any form of addiction (e.g. smoking, alcohol, drugs).

7. Techniques for controlled super-effective relaxation and sleep.

8. Techniques to allow choice of sex and other characteristics of unborn children.

9. The postponement of aging along with limited rejuvenation and improved cosmetic surgery.

10. New prevention techniques utilizing holistic health approaches and environmental control.

11. Expanded use of psychotechnologies (e.g., psychotherapies, meditation, yoga, biofeedback, dream analysis) and development of new techniques for self-management of lifestyle.

12. New diagnostic procedures (CAT-scan, angiogram) and surgical procedures (angioplasty).

13. Expanded use of ovum and sperm banks.

14. Improvement of "The Opticon" will totally replace Braille for the blind. This is a machine that allows a blind person to move a camera over any printed material while his/her index finger follows on an electronic pad the patterns of letters and words (in English not Braille).

15. Improvement of the Kurzweil Reading Machine, which "reads" any English written material and simultaneously translates it into a "human voice" read-out; there are also talking calculators.

16. An electrocardiogram belt, worn anywhere except in the tub or shower, that constantly monitors heartbeat and other vital signs.

17. An artificial pancreas, a monitoring and dispensing device that measures blood sugar level and dispenses doses of insulin.

18. New immunological vaccines and other controls for disease.

19. New techniques of brain stimulation to control pain, eliminate paralysis, and modify and control self-destructive behaviors.

20. Artificial wombs, fluid baths in which animal and human fetuses can be kept alive and nurtured through "birth."

21. Bone marrow transplants to prevent and/or cure leukemia, bone cancer, and anemia.

22. Cloning or parthenogenesis, which is using a cell (not an egg or sperm) from one organism to create genetically identical organisms.

23. A variety of human-computer interfaces to control brain deficiencies and improve memory and intelligence.

24. Brain transplants by keeping brains alive outside the body during the lengthy surgical procedure.

25. Regeneration of human body parts in much the same way lizards and worms regenerate limbs and segments.

26. Since cancer researchers have just determined that it is highly unlikely we can ever eradicate cancer in all its many forms, we can still learn how to catch it and control it in its early stages.

Undoubtedly, the next century will see the bionic human become a reality, as is dramatically portrayed in Figure 5.

The results of medical developments will undoubtedly be increased life expectancy (at birth) from 70 years, to 100 years, to perhaps 150 years—even immortality is possible. Without other future developments, however, the question to be asked is: What quality of existence will a person experience in a lifetime of 150 or 200 years or one that extends forever?

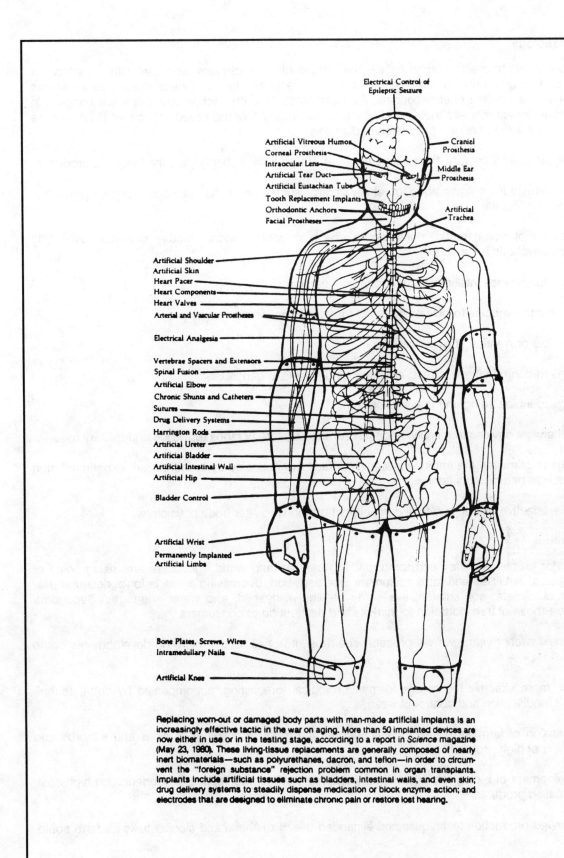

Electrical Control of
Epileptic Seizure

Artificial Vitreous Humor
Corneal Prosthesis
Intraocular Lens
Artificial Tear Duct
Artificial Eustachian Tube
Tooth Replacement Implants
Orthodontic Anchors
Facial Prostheses

Cranial
Prosthesis

Middle Ear
Prosthesis

Artificial
Trachea

Artificial Shoulder
Artificial Skin
Heart Pacer
Heart Components
Heart Valves
Arterial and Vascular Prostheses

Electrical Analgesia

Vertebrae Spacers and Extensors
Spinal Fusion
Artificial Elbow
Chronic Shunts and Catheters
Sutures
Drug Delivery Systems
Harrington Rods
Artificial Ureter
Artificial Bladder
Artificial Intestinal Wall
Artificial Hip

Bladder Control

Artificial Wrist
Permanently Implanted
Artificial Limbs

Bone Plates, Screws, Wires
Intramedullary Nails

Artificial Knee

Replacing worn-out or damaged body parts with man-made artificial implants is an
increasingly effective tactic in the war on aging. More than 50 implanted devices are
now either in use or in the testing stage, according to a report in *Science* magazine
(May 23, 1980). These living-tissue replacements are generally composed of nearly
inert biomaterials—such as polyurethanes, dacron, and teflon—in order to circum-
vent the "foreign substance" rejection problem common in organ transplants.
Implants include artificial tissues such as bladders, intestinal walls, and even skin;
drug delivery systems to steadily dispense medication or block enzyme action; and
electrodes that are designed to eliminate chronic pain or restore lost hearing.

Figure 5. The bionic human[96]

Pharmacology

The companion to medical technology is the work of pharmacologists, who deal with the effects of chemicals and drugs on the human organism and who create and test a range of drugs and medicines that comprise the modern pharmacopoeia. As in the case of every technology, there are dangers in chemico-technologies, namely the side effects and secondary (often delayed) effects of drugs whose primary effects are the cure or amelioration of diseases.

For the twenty-first century, the science of pharmacology will probably yield the following products:

1. Improvement in contraceptives for fertility control, such as oral and male contraceptive pills effective for weeks or months.

2. Creation of non-narcotic, nonaddictive drugs to control and/or modify behavior, especially neurotic and psychotic behaviors.

3. Drugs to enhance intelligence, memory, and learning.

4. Birth control vaccine to obviate the need for vasectomy or ovariectomy.

5. Chemical prevention of hypertension.

6. Drugs to control fatigue, stress, alertness, and moods in general.

7. Drugs to inhibit aging and prevent senility.

8. Biochemical devices to identify, trace, and/or incapacitate persons for police and military uses.

9. Drugs to stimulate the immune system to attack malignancies as in the current experimentation with interferon, a natural virus-fighter.

10. Safe, effective use of growth and inhibitory hormones to alter body physiology.

Agriculture

The major problems, today and tomorrow, in American and world agriculture are: rising costs of petroleum-based fertilizers and farm equipment, soil depletion, decreasing acreage for agricultural use, uncertainty of climate, soil erosion, availability of high-yield seed, and water shortages. Secondary problems are those of transportation to markets and distribution to consumers.

In the next twenty years, we will probably see most, if not all, of the following developments come to fruition:

1. New, more effective techniques for meteorological forecasting, accompanied by better techniques for the modification and control of weather.

2. Expansion of farming to new locales such as the roofs of buildings in cities and suburbs and ocean farming of high protein fish.

3. Development of biological, organic, nonfossil fuel fertilizers to reduce dependence on high-cost, petroleum-based products.

4. Improved production techniques and expanded use of methane and alcohol fuels for farm equipment.

5. Less expensive methods for the desalination of sea water to make it possible to irrigate previously "useless" land.

6. Creation of plants that make their own fertilizer.

7. Improved hybrid seeds coupled with genetically recombined new species of seed to increase per-acre yields.

8. Automated factories for the raising and processing of poultry and fish.

9. Computer-controlled farming, as a farm is conceived of as a self-contained ecosystem in which water and nutrients are constantly recycled.

10. Creation of some new plant species that grow in salty soil, or that are hardy perennials blooming yearly without replanting, or that yield several harvests per growing season.

11. Change of human diets to incorporate more nutritious, high protein foods such as rabbit and beefalo.

12. New, more effective techniques for storage, conservation, and recycling of water.

13. Improved techniques of food preservation, storage, compressed packaging, and cooled/heated transportation units.

14. Computers in almost all homes to permit remote buying of supermarket products, which will also save supermarket space and the cost of shelf displays and advertising.

Automation/Robots

With the advent of automation and robots, the abolition of strenuous, tedious work has become a technological possibility. Already, most of us are familiar with welding robots in automobile plants and robot toys on wheels with wire sensors. Automation is a process applied to machines, whereby they become self-correcting through the use of information feedback and have the capacity to adjust themselves. Automation is enhanced by hooking the machine to a computer, allowing for response to hundreds or thousands of contingencies.

A robot is any creation by a human (or by another robot) that is able to sense, to decide, and to act. Its potential for making decisions and for complicated actions is multiplied by incorporating computers in its design.

The greatest economic potential for automation and robots in the near future appears to lie in three sectors of the market: industrial productivity, replacing workers in hazardous occupations, and recreational toys. Probably somewhat later, reasonably priced household robots will appear as mass-produced gadgets.

At present, there are about 18,000 robots at work in Japanese factories and about 7,000 in United States factories. They perform an array of manufacturing functions such as grinding, cutting, welding, fitting, performing quality checks, and moving inventories from place to place in warehouses. A new generation of mobile robots will soon be working in environments hazardous to (even hostile to) human life, such as in mines, in tunnels, on skyscrapers, and underwater. In the next century, robots will fix gas leaks, cap oil wells, handle radioactive materials, and even build space stations.

Energy

"Ten years after the Arab oil embargo, the goal of 'energy independence' remains as elusive as ever. The United States continues to import some six million barrels of oil a day, sending $60 billion abroad every year."[97] Although amount of oil consumed and cost per barrel are important factors, the overarching issue is how the nations of the world will power their societies in the future. At least three dichotomies comprise this issue: use/non-use (i.e., conservation), near-term future/distant future (i.e., depletion vis-a-vis time), and nonrenewable energy sources/renewable energy sources (i.e., availability and pollution effects).

In the United States, excessive reliance on petroleum will change gradually over the next 20 or 30 years to a combination of multiple energy sources, both nonrenewable and renewable. In the short term, the transition period, probably not more than 15 or 20 years, we will continue to rely heavily on oil and gas, modified by improvements in efficiency (in engines, furnaces, ranges, etc.); by increased conservation efforts (spurred by higher prices and educational efforts); and by greater reliance on coal, nuclear power (fission), synthetic fuels (e.g., gasahol and methanol), and numerous types of solar energy (e.g., rays, wind, tides). Table 9 shows our pattern of energy consumption in 1981.

Table 9
Energy Consumption in 1981

Oil (Barrels per Day)	15.9 million
Gas (Cubic Feet)	19.6 trillion
Coal (Tons)	729 million
Nuclear (Btu)	2.9 quadrillion
Synthetics (Barrels per Day)	0
Solar and other renewables (Btu)	4.8 quadrillion
Total Energy Use (Btu)	75.7 quadrillion

By 2000, it is estimated that our total energy use will be 97 quadrillion Btu's, with oil declining to 13.7 million barrels per day, coal and solar doubling, nuclear tripling, synthetics increasing to about 1.25 million barrels per day, and natural gas remaining constant.[98]

But what about long-range prospects? Most estimates of the supply and use of oil and gas lead to the conclusion that by 2050, negligible reserves of these fossil fuels will remain. By this time Americans will be using coal, hydroelectric power, synthetic fuels, both fission and fusion nuclear energy, and numerous forms of solar power: solar panels, windmills, rising and falling tides, photovoltaic cells, and even gigantic solar collectors in geostationary orbit in space. And of course conservation in the forms of non-use and improved efficiency will still be a crucial variable in the new complex energy formula.

Transportation

What is involved in the category of transportation are the movement of people and goods on Earth and in space, short hauls and long hauls, commuting, and business and recreational travel. In the future, the individual may have transportation needs that begin at a point on the Earth's surface, for example, a home near the University of Colorado campus in Boulder, Colorado. From this point, one needs to get to work and to various commercial locations, such as supermarkets, downtown, and shopping malls. Although this Coloradan could reach these destinations by walking, by bicycle, or by shuttle bus, he/she typically uses the automobile, exemplifying Americans' love affair with their private autos. Any transportation future for the United States must take into account this psychological phenomenon. Thus, the transportation matrix contain more than technological factors; it includes psychological, sociological, and educational variables as well. Merely improving the efficiency of the internal combustion engine will not suffice, although increasing the miles per gallon of four-cylinder car engines to 75-100 miles per gallon will alleviate depletion and cost problems. What also will be needed are personal and social changes that yield receptivity to alternative modes of transportation, especially to multiple types of public transportation.

Not infrequently our Coloradan wants to take advantage of the many cultural and other services only available in the urban metropolis of Denver, 30 miles away. Again, laziness and convenience combine to favor the family car, although downtown Denver traffic and the cost of parking cause some to question the wisdom of avoiding the RTD bus. If the RTD board of directors has its way, Denver and the surrounding metropolitan area may soon be served by a type of ground-level or elevated fixed-rail system, in addition to or as a substitute for existing buses.

What if the Coloradan needs, for business purposes, to travel to Chicago, or New York, or Los Angeles? AMTRAK is too slow and offers few of the amenities formerly provided on trains. Hence, the inevitable answer is air transportation. But our business traveler must begin such a trip from home and thus must make some arrangement to get to the Denver airport from Boulder and to reverse the procedure at the end of the trip. If the flight destination is the JFK terminal in New York City, our business traveler is again faced with ground transportation into the city and out again after concluding his/her business. These two flights and the related four ground trips might be tolerable requirements for conducting some types of business, but when they are combined with other stressful and often inconvenient conditions, business travel becomes an unwelcome chore. Planes today mesh cramped seats (six across and restricted leg room) with near-capacity loads, making two-to-four-hour trips uncomfortable for all the passengers. Airport parking at large city terminals is now to the point that in order to be assured a space at a reasonable rate, one must park off the airport property up to a mile or two away. Further, buses and shuttle buses (or airport limousines for the wealthier) are often crowded, scheduled inconveniently, and present a formidable challenge for anyone with much baggage. Airports themselves are now crowded, with overpriced goods and services, and long check-in lines. If this situation is discouraging, consider the obstacles in air travel for the family embarking on a vacation.

Of course business and tourism today are not limited to travel within the borders of a single nation. All the world is a market and everyone is an international tourist, at least potentially. There is even a polar route, an eight-hour, non-stop flight between Denver and Frankfurt, West Germany. As aircraft speeds increase, however, they are accompanied by fuel pollution, noise pollution, and excessive consumption of fuel, to the point that, at least in the United States, the development of the supersonic transport was halted by Congress. The French-United Kingdom *Concorde* is allowed to land only at airports that are approached from the ocean. But clearly in another sense we do have a supersonic "plane" in the successes of NASA's space shuttle.

All the above modes of transportation already exist, so what can we expect in the next 20 years or so? The following developments are likely by the year 2000:

1. Four-cylinder car engines that get 100 miles per gallon or more.

2. Improved bullet trains (like some that exist now in Japan and West Germany), suspended on electromagnetic cushions just above power rails, that move at speeds of 300 miles per gallon or more.

3. Smaller, safer cars.

4. Some electric cars for short commutes; recharging of batteries at home or in specially equipped city parking garages, all during late night hours.

5. In big cities, more subways, trolleys, and "moving sidewalks" (like some of the current moving ramps in airport concourses).

6. Some drone vehicles (pilotless, driverless, conductorless, etc.) — trains, subways, mine trains, warehouse forklift trucks, and cars.

Space Travel/Colonies

The human animal seems driven to surmount seemingly impossible challenges—to capture the "magic" of lightning in fire, to move over the Earth faster than any other animal, to construct buildings taller than any tree, to fly like the birds yet faster and higher, and to even overcome our Earthbound nature by creating homes in space. Given the implacable obstacles, what remarkable achievements the human species has realized. How can we not expect that in some future we will roam and make the entire universe our home?

But what is reasonable to expect in the next two or three decades? With our many pressing problems of keeping our home planet habitable and the increasing costs of launching space vehicles, the world's nations can give only limited financial reserves to the monumental efforts of space travel and colonization; but this is true only in the short run. The moral imperative of social justice and stewardship in combination with unforeseen obstacles and a modicum of humility will leave many challenges for our children's grandchildren and their children in our inexorable space odyssey. By the year 2010 (in honor of Arthur C. Clarke), we can expect the following events:

1. Increased commercial (nondefense) chartering of the space shuttle by U.S. and foreign corporations to further investigate the economic potential of near space and the Moon and to launch from the shuttle numerous new communications satellites.

2. A semipermanent, manned spacelab in geosynchronous orbit to conduct basic and applied research; perhaps as many as three labs, one each over the Soviet Union, Western Europe, and the United States.

3. Further exploration of our solar system, of a few of the planets and their moons, by manned and unmanned probes.

4. A few scheduled flights of the space shuttle reserved for rather expensive prestige tourism; the equivalent for the rich of a "Sunday drive in the country."

5. Perhaps a small prototype space colony located equidistant between the Earth and the Moon, with a primary purpose of gathering solar energy in huge, flexible panels to, in turn, be beamed back to power stations on Earth.

Missing from this section on space, and from all the previous categories of technological developments, is the uncongenial topic of weapons technologies, including nuclear devices, their missile delivery vehicles, land and ocean launch sites, "conventional" weapons, orbiting reconnaissance satellites, and the general militarization of space. With current levels of military expenditures worldwide, ample funds are available to create the means for numerous unimaginable holocausts. If present levels of funding continue through the end of the century (increases are more likely), weapons specialists will probably develop many if not all of the following weapons technologies:

1. Lethal and incapacitating biochemical agents.

2. Laser and maser beam rifles and cannons.

3. Superhelicopters for airborne infantry and artillery.

4. More effective brainwashing techniques.

5. Less expensive and more mobile nuclear devices.

6. Space "defense" systems, beginning with antisatellite missiles.

7. Greater accuracy of nuclear delivery systems.

8. Battlefield electronic surveillance, camouflage, and evasion.

9. Increased range of artillery shells propelled by electromagnetic "mass movers."

10. Space-based nuclear weapons (currently prohibited by SALT).

Ironically and fortunately, the history of war and the development of lethal weapons have frequently led to benign applications and peacetime uses. It is difficult today, however, to envision benefits to humankind deriving out of nuclear war.

Communications

One way of defining technology is to consider it as the variety of means, modes, or techniques for *extending* the power or influence of the human being. For example, a bow and arrow *extends* the range of the human arm, which is not capable of throwing a projectile as hard and far as the bow catapults the arrow. Or, as another example, the automobile *extends* the speed and range of human mobility; that is, a person cannot walk or run as far or as fast as one can using a car. In the domain of communications, technologies *extend* the abilities of hearing, speech, memory, sight, thinking, and other human communication capabilities. For example, the telegraph and Morse code (the first a "hard" technology and the latter a "soft" one) extend the range of the human voice and human language, albeit in coded form. The telephone was the logical successor to the telegraph. Communication technologies have historically evolved from language to tom-toms, smoke signals, and megaphones; to writing and the printing press; to telegraph and telephone; to radio, television, and communication satellites. In this century, the evolution of calculators—abacus, mechanical calculators, electronic calculators, computers—has merged with the history of communication techniques. Thus, today we have a complex of natural, machine, and synthetic languages, of audio and visual devices (wired and wireless), and of slow/fast, small/large, and minimum memory/extensive memory computers.

If we are currently in the Communications Revolution, it is because of the potential for communication systems (multiple combinations of techniques and devices) that can be derived from combining the following:

1. Telephone (handsets, copper and fiber-optic cable, electronic switching equipment, microwave transmission and relay stations).

2. Radio (AM and FM transmission to home and car receivers).

3. Television (black-and-white and color, wireless and cable, laserdisc and VCR, commercial discs and cassettes).

4. Computers (large mainframes, minis and micros, processing speed and memory capacity, disks and diskettes, monochrome and color monitors, software programs, *and the capability to interface with and control all the above hardware and software*).

5. A worldwide electric power grid that permits use of all the above devices by almost anyone, almost anywhere.

6. Space-based communication satellites that permit wireless transmission from almost anywhere to almost anywhere else.

The importance of the computer in communications is its capability to control (by interfaces and interactions) multiple modes of communication (i.e., systems) with incredible speed and precision.

The future of communication technologies holds the promise of:

1. Improvements in computers: smaller units, faster performance, greater memory capacity, more functions, and wider applications.

2. Improvements in television: smaller units, bigger screens, smaller VCRs and more types of cassettes available, more on-the-air channels as well as cable channels (up to 100 or more).

3. Expanded "electronic marketing": postal service, shopping for groceries and other products, banking, publishing of books, newspapers, magazines, and journals, bills and advertising, and bartering of information and products.

4. Expanded uses for remote control (wireless as in current use with television sets and VCRs) and perfection of voice-activated equipment such as typewriters and tape recorders.

5. Improved artificial intelligence (via computers and in robots with voice synthesizers).

These developments, and many of those in other categories, will undoubtedly have dramatic impacts on how humans exist and interact in the home, the workplace, and in educational institutions.

Assuming that private and public schools at all levels—from preschools to universities and other continuing education institutions—will continue to exist for at least the next 25 years, how will these places of learning be affected by the new communication technologies? In regard to computers, Decker Walker of Stanford University states: "My experience—derived from three years of reading, thinking, and working with computers and computer-based education programs—leads me to identify seven main ways that today's microcomputers can contribute to education. These are: (1) more active learning, (2) more varied sensory and conceptual modes, (3) less mental drudgery, (4) learning nearer the speed of thought, (5) learning better tailored to individuals, (6) more independent learning, and (7) better aids to abstraction."[99]

As a "teacher," the computer can manage the instructional process, can construct and analyze tests, and can be an interactive tutor. Computers can be aids to motivating students to learn, can aid both teachers and students in developing problem-solving skills, and can aid in the many routines and records of classroom management. But perhaps the greatest potential use of the computer is as the manager of peripheral devices (sometimes called Interactive Computer-Assisted Instruction) such as printers, VCRs, slide projectors, and the like.

The Domain of Social Issues

One futurist has called our present predicament a "crisis of crises," which emphasizes the complexity and interrelatedness of concurrent crises.[100]

Those individual crises that comprise the megacrisis are variously named and described by different authors. Lester Brown views the megacrises from the perspective of an ecologist. For Brown, these are the issues:[101]

1. The carrying capacity of the planet.

2. The "Tragedy of the Commons" (i.e., the dilemma that self-interest pays off when the individual uses up as much of the social common stock as he or she is allowed before using his or her own private stock).

    a. Overfishing the ocean "commons."

    b. Deforestation of the forest "commons."

    c. Overgrazing.

    d. Overplowing.

    e. Overloading air, water, and land (e.g., pollution).

3. Consequences of No. 2:

    a. Loss of cropland and erosion.

    b. Polluted oceans ("the ultimate sink").

    c. Endangered species.

    d. Environmentally induced illnesses.

    e. Inadvertent climate change and natural disasters.

4. The overpopulation threat.

5. The depletion of energy resources.

6. The food shortage (and attendant problems of shortage of arable land and pollution caused by fertilizers).

7. The economic sphere: unemployment, inflation, scarce capital, and diminishing returns.

8. The unequal distribution of wealth within and between nations, and absolute and relative poverty.

9. The advantages and problems of technology.

10. The problems of accommodation and social change.

Willis Harman talks about the "five fundamental failures of the industrial era paradigm." The industrial paradigm encompasses industrialization, science, materialism, and pragmatism (utilitarianism plus hedonism). The five failures of the paradigm are:[102]

1. Failure to provide individuals with opportunities to contribute to society and to be affirmed by society in return (i.e., problems of personal alienation and efficacy).

2. Failure to foster equitable distribution of power and justice (i.e., the problems of socioeconomic classes and of rich and poor nations).

3. Failure to foster responsible technology management.

4. Failure to provide goals and visions capable of attracting loyalties and commitments (i.e., the problem of a lack of positive and compelling images of the future).

5. Failure to maintain the habitability of the planet.

Finally, this writer has developed two lists of global problems: the first includes problems at the surface in global societies—physical, material, economic, political problems; and the second lists problems that lie beneath the surface of a society—consciousness, cultural, infrastructural problems. The first list is termed "Societal Problems" and the second, "Cultural Problems."[103]

Societal Problems

1. Hunger and inadequate nutrition: starvation.

2. Depletion of natural resources: arable land, water, air, and fossil fuels.

3. Extinction of plant and animal species.

4. Inequality—between nations and within a single nation—of material wealth, risk capital, and natural resources.

5. Overpopulation by nation, region, or urban area.

6. Economic imperialism: rich nations exploiting poorer nations.

7. Threat of wars: nuclear, "acquisition," and/or "redistribution."

8. Plagues, other diseases, and inadequate medical care.

9. Environmental degradation: pollution, waste disposal, etc.

10. Crime and other violations of human and property rights.

11. Shortages: of medicines, foods, energy, fertilizers, etc.

12. Economic malfunctions: depression, recession, unemployment, inflation.

13. Credibility gaps: between and among politicians, scientists, business leaders, and citizens.

14. Illiteracy, overschooling, and overspecialization.

15. Guerrilla warfare, terrorism, and other forms of violent aggression.

16. Social pathologies: superaffluence, conspicuous consumption, and "demonstration effects."

Cultural Problems

1. The absence of powerful substitutes for the waning belief systems of Christianity, Marxism, and Primitivism.

2. The lack of alternatives to addiction to growth and naive faith in technology magic.

3. The dilemmas of dualisms, as between intellect and feelings, analysis and commitment, and ends and means.

4. The need for a more humane cosmology other than mechanical and mathematical reductionisms.

5. The tacit acceptance of a cynical drift in human affairs.

6. The tendency toward rampant hedonism, myopic presentism, and unbridled individualism.

7. The lack of positive and hopeful symbols and dreams of global, communal, conjoint living.

8. The absence of universal, species-wide myths and epics.

9. The tendency to avoid the future, to drive into the future with one's eyes firmly riveted on the rearview mirror, the past.

10. The lack of a collective will to act when action is necessary.

What is clear from these lists is that, although local manifestations may vary, these issues pervade our globe; they are complex due to the interdependent nature of all modern nation-states; they are all interwoven, making it difficult, if not impossible, to deal with one in isolation from the others; and they are long-term, destined to be with us for at least the next 25 years.

With respect to the crisis of crises, one other characteristic of this web of issues is crucial. Although we enjoy closure, the satisfaction of solving a problem, the very nature of contemporary social issues causes them to resist total solution or else to yield a solution that in turn leads to a new problem.

3. PROBING THE FUTURE

The study of the future, like any other discipline of knowledge, has its own frames of reference and research techniques. Futurology, however, also borrows freely from other subjects, such as history, sociology (and other social sciences), and literature. Most of all, futurists by and large are generalists who range across the many landscapes of reality.

Futurists vary incredibly in the modes of "knowing" they use to probe and discover the future. From the creative literary approaches, such as utopias (and of course their opposite, "dystopias") and science fiction to the technology assessment techniques used by the Rand Corporation, futurists invent facts and data or rigorously apply rules of evidence, depending on their needs and inclinations. Thus, in futurology there is a place for the artist and the scientist, for flights of imagination and for intensely practical applications to public policy—even for the mystic and the psychic.

Ways of learning about the future will probably comprise many of the frontier research methods in the next half century. Currently, the modes of investigation used by futurists can be categorized as follows: genius forecasting, trend extrapolation, consensus methods, cross-impact matrix.

Genius Forecasting

This method of "creating" the future is used by at least three kinds of futurists: novelists and writers of science fiction, creators of utopias, and well-informed and highly intuitive scientists and other scholars. Among the novelists and science fiction writers are Jules Verne, H.G. Wells, Aldous Huxley, George Orwell, Robert Heinlein, Ray Bradbury, Michael Crichton, and Frank Herbert. Some of the creators of utopias are B.F. Skinner, Edward Bellamy, Plato, Thomas More, plus a few authors from the first list. Scientists and scholars include Herman Kahn, Marquis de Condorcet, Alvin Toffler, some from the previous lists, and at least two individuals who represent all types—Arthur C. Clarke and Isaac Asimov.

Because of the interplay of creative, intuitive, and analytic capacities employed by these forecasters, it is somewhat difficult to describe the method of genius forecasting. There are, nevertheless, some characteristics of this technique that can be identified. One feature is the "leap to a date" sometime in the future—ten or twenty years hence, or even a hundred or a thousand years into the future. This is generally a leap that ignores how we get from here, the present, to there, a time in the future. A second aspect of this approach is the use of literary devices like plot and characterization, ways of personalizing the future scenario and giving it a story line. Third is the depiction of an ideal social milieu, a utopia, or its opposite, a dystopia as in George Orwell's *1984*. Finally, there is the resort to using exotic scientific "discoveries" and spectacular technological creations, which tend to promote dramatic "revolutions" in personal and societal modes of living.

Trend Extrapolation

This approach consists of the extension of historical and present patterns into the future. It is basically a conservative, evolutionary mode of forecasting, which assumes continuous, linear, unidirectional movement from past to present to future, without the intervention of surprises or crises. The forces that were at work to shape the trend in the past will continue to work in the future. Although not limited to such evidence, much trend extrapolation relies on quantitative data—especially economic and demographic statistics. For example, Figure 6 is typical of statistical trend extrapolation, in this case a projection of world population growth by regions to the year 2000.

Future History

The reconstruction of the past is based on the evidence that has survived and is available to the historian, and also on the ability and creativity of the writer of history. There is one past, but many histories; and there will be a single future, though many future histories.

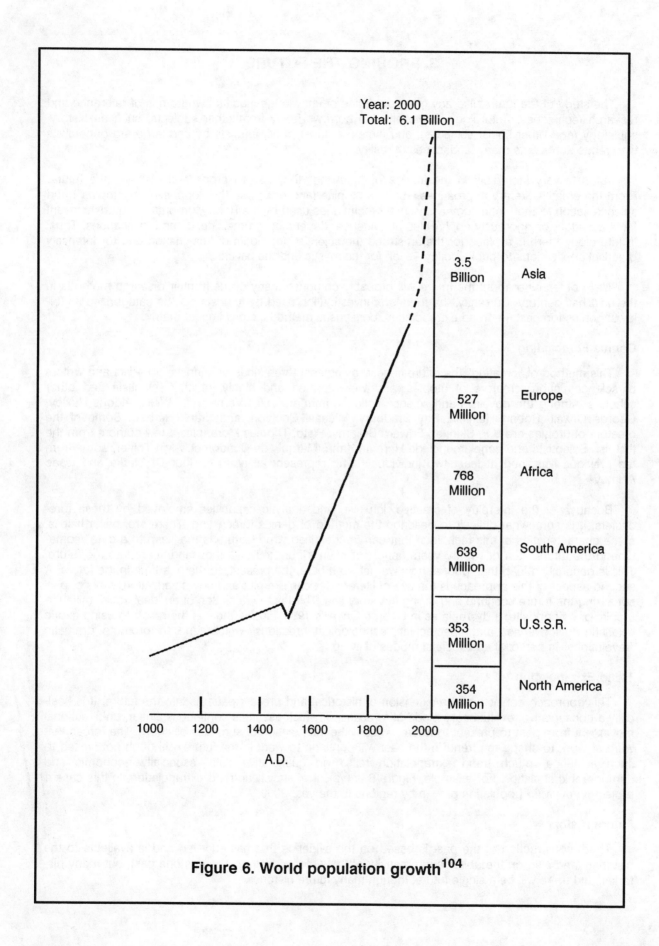

Year: 2000
Total: 6.1 Billion

3.5 Billion — Asia

527 Million — Europe

768 Million — Africa

638 Million — South America

353 Million — U.S.S.R.

354 Million — North America

1000 1200 1400 1600 1800 2000

A.D.

Figure 6. World population growth[104]

In constructing a future history, the futurist relies on many perspectives: a familiarity with histories of the past, a sound analysis of the present, imagination tempered by cautiousness, and a sense of time flow. There are at least two formats used in creating future history: (1) postulating a future event and then flashing back to the present or recent past to trace the sequence from past to present to future event, and (2) beginning in the past or present and "playing out" a plausible future.

The historian of the future may choose to focus on continuity or change, on cycles or "pendulum swings," on leadership initiative or sociocultural determinism, and on any of the many topics or subjects available to historians in general. The final product is a history, a narrative account of a sequence of events or trends over time, anchored in past and/or present facts and extending into the future.

In the field of education, future histories are rare, but one can gain some sense of how future history reads from the following two fragments of societal futures:

> During the winter of 1986, Russia began marching toward Baluchistan and the Abadan oil fields, only recently restored to full production since the Iraqi war. This action followed increasing tension between NATO and the Soviets due to Russian insistence that East Germany discontinue unification talks with West Germany. Chinese troops engaged in their most serious conflict to date on their northern border. Soviet troops had invaded at the Dzungarian Gate, using tanks and anti-personnel weapons on the Chinese troops. On the Pacific, the seizure of Japanese fishing trawlers had Japan, Korea, and the U.S. vigorously protesting Soviet extension of its maritime boundaries. Russia seemed to have reached its most irritable and unpredictable state. While Russia saw itself surrounded by an increasingly hostile world, the world saw itself threatened by an increasingly hostile Russia. Stories coming from Russia reported that there were severe shortages of meat, butter, and staples like cooking oil. Embassy officials in Moscow reported long queues at bakeries. There were unconfirmed reports of internal sabotage by Shiite Muslims at the Azerbaidzan oil fields.
>
> At home the fourth credit crunch in eight years coincided with the worst winter in eighty. With low oil stocks and soaring interest rates, financial liquidity reached its lowest point, both for individuals and for corporations. Defaults in small savings and loan institutions were followed by bankruptcies of restaurants, stores, supermarkets, and small manufacturing concerns. The rash of bankruptcies would have become a torrent had the government not extended loans through the newly reconstituted Reconstruction Finance Agency.
>
> Meanwhile the price of gold soared as riots in Soweto threatened to engulf South Africa in a protracted racial war. Mideast tensions, chronic oil shortages, Russian bellowing, and near economic chaos in financial markets drove people into panicky financial decisions. At gold's peak of $2,255 an ounce, people weren't sure whether to sell their fillings and get cash, or sell their possessions to buy gold. They did both in a state of rapid and utter confusion. Thefts increased, silver disappeared from china cabinets, hearing aid batteries were stolen from the ears of the elderly (each contained $50 worth of silver), and jewelry stores bolted their doors and posted signs: By Appointment Only.[105]

> By the early 1980s, $5 billion had been earmarked for the development of a synthetic fuels program which promised 1.5 million barrels of synthetic fuels per day, primarily from Western coal liquifaction. A major pipeline system to divert Mississippi River water to the Rockies was under construction to provide the needed water for the liquifaction process. This system eased the demand on limited water supplies in Western states already stretched to the limits by urban and agricultural uses.

"Boom towns" were springing up in Colorado and Wyoming as coal conversion plants were constructed near the coal sites. Erecting these plants near the source reduced the transportation demands of this new technology and increased the net energy produced through the process. Problems associated with "boom town" syndrome such as the necessarily increased demands for housing, social services and water were frequently noted by social planners but went unaddressed.

This energy upheaval in the mid-1980s resulted in further strains on the economy, so that midway through the decade domestic industries clamored for relief from less expensive imports. Quotas and tariffs, reduced through international agreements only five years earlier, reappeared to protect threatened industries. The international community responded in kind, so that eventually developing countries, the major purchasers of American goods, were forced to pay more and receive less. This did nothing to enhance American global prestige.

The failure to reach national economic goals was likewise due to periodic worldwide bouts with poor weather, which caused a tightening of food supplies and higher prices. Because of the climatic changes for the worse during the 1980s, several countries, including the Soviet Union and its Eastern block satellites, having become accustomed to more meat in their diets, substantially increased their wheat and corn purchases. The U.S., mindful of the beneficial with these ever increasing orders. Grains which remained in America were thus more expensive because of the heightened demand and because of the increased costs of production, especially for petroleum-based fertilizers, and higher water costs.

By the 1980s, a serious battle for water had developed among agricultural, industrial and urban consumers. Agriculturalists and industrialists both argued for increased water rights to enhance productivity while governors, especially in the Western states, faced the problem of providing water for the rapidly growing cities situated in generally arid regions. Coastal cities experimented with large-scale desalinization plants, although as an energy-intensive process, it created further strains on the economy.

The newspapers were already devoting extensive coverage to the expected completion of 40 nuclear power stations coming on line in 1992. The economy, while nowhere near fully recovered, was progressing upward satisfactorily with increasing use of liquified and gasified coal.

In October, 1991, however, inhabitants of Western states awoke one morning to learn that the Dresden-2 boiler water reactor near Chicago had suffered a major loss of coolant when the pressure control system malfunctioned. Two-and-one-half million people living within a ten-mile radius of the plant were in the process of being evacuated. Roads were jammed, multiple accidents had further slowed the evacuation process, and a state of emergency was declared by the Governor of Illinois. Radioactivity was released from the containment building for three days before operators were able to contain the leakage. Those who had evacuated were forced to leave their homes for one month while 12-hour checks were made on the level of radioactivity in the environs.[106]

Another possible future history might be that of an urban high school. The "Future Wheel" in Figure 7 indicates the potential directions a short-term future history might take.

Decision Trees

A decision tree is a pictorial representation of the potential results of alternative approaches to crucial decisions. It is a futures methodology likening to a tree—with a trunk and main and subsidiary branches—a range and sequence of decision points, over time, and in relation to a goal or future situa

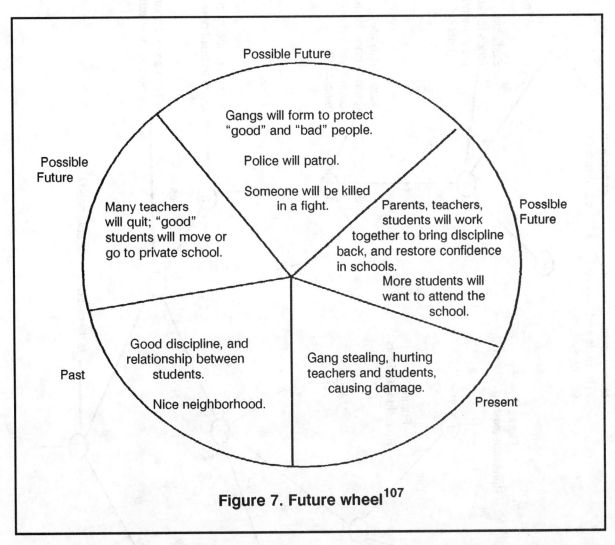

Possible Future

Gangs will form to protect "good" and "bad" people.

Police will patrol.

Someone will be killed in a fight.

Possible Future

Many teachers will quit; "good" students will move or go to private school.

Parents, teachers, students will work together to bring discipline back, and restore confidence in schools.

More students will want to attend the school.

Possible Future

Good discipline, and relationship between students.

Nice neighborhood.

Gang stealing, hurting teachers and students, causing damage.

Past

Present

Figure 7. Future wheel[107]

tion. Decision trees are constructed in either the "growing tall" variety or the "cut down" version. The "growing tall" type appears to "grow" vertically from the bottom of a sheet of paper toward the top, with a thick trunk at the bottom and subsidiary branches extending toward the right edge, with the time continuum progressing horizontally from left (earliest dates) to right (furthest future dates). The "cut down" version lies on its side in a horizontal mode, with decision points extending from left (trunk and roots) to right (upper branches).

In Figure 8, the "growing tall" type of decision tree yields six discrete alternative futures (Futures A, B, C, D, E, and F), which might emerge from the various responses to decision point questions. Of these six futures, two (E and F) reflect an affirmative response to the question "Should we build a new high school?"; four (A, B, C, and D) are negative response options. In this example, the decision tree technique is used for deriving rather short-range alternative futures for an educational question. If our question were, "Should we develop and use biochemical products (drugs) to improve the learning achievement of public school students?," our decision tree would be more complicated and would involve a long-range timeline. It is probable that such a tree would have to be mapped and contained in a computer.

Cross-Impact Matrix Analysis

This method is designed to take into account the fact that a human event has multiple causes and both intended and unintended effects. "This interrelationship between events and developments is

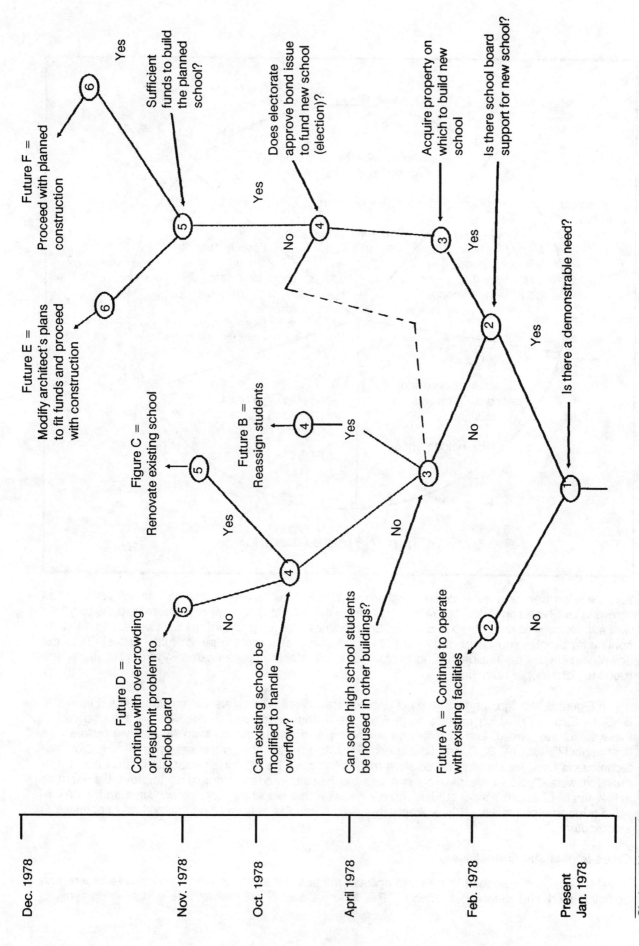

Figure 8. Decision Tree for the Question, "Should we build a new high school?"

Circles with numbers inside represent decision points.

called 'cross-impact.'"[108] This technique also reveals probable new problems that are often created when another problem is "solved." For example, when medical science found ways of decreasing infant mortality rates and prolonging life expectancy, it created other problems of overpopulation and geriatric care. Or, the technologies developed and used to build automated factories also caused an increase in unemployment and obsolescence of certain human skills.

Although the process of a cross-impact analysis is rather complex as a futures research methodology, it can be readily understood from a simple everyday situation. A young woman of 17, when asked about her goals for the next few years, declared that she wanted to travel some, to improve her swimming skills so that she could compete in meets, and to attend a quality college. Realizing the factor of time involved in all three activities, she used a form of cross-impact matrix in order to "see" how each goal impinged on the other two. Table 10 represents the young woman's analysis of the interrelationships involved in the simultaneous pursuit of all three of her goals. It also serves as an example of a cross-impact matrix.

Table 10
A Cross-Impact Matrix Analysis[109]

Personal Goals	Personal Goals		
How Will This Goal → Affect This Goal? ↓	To travel	To improve swimming skills	To attend a quality college
To travel	X	Except for "off-season" times, swimming would preclude travel	College work will preempt about nine months, restricting travel to summers and holidays
To improve swimming skills	Any extended travel might interfere with training and meet schedules	X	Course work at a quality college may restrict extra-curricular activities like swimming
To attend a quality college	Except for summers, holidays, or semester leaves of absence, travel would preclude college	Due to rigorous training and heavy meet schedule, swimming might interfere with college	X

The cross-impact matrix analysis method can also be applied to educational futures, as in the five-event interaction portrayed in Table 11. Here, one postulates that the events numbered 1 through 5 will occur at some future time, say from 1976 to 2000. A computer is used to manipulate the data derived from a group of research subjects or participants in order to obtain information about probability of occurrence of each event, and, if an event were to occur, its probable effect on each of the other four events. Inputs would include trend data and estimates of both occurrence and impact. In Table 11, the impact of event upon event is displayed in the five-by-five matrix at the far right of the table. These impact estimates were derived by having subjects judge the degree of impact according to a scale from −10 to +10, where −10 indicates that a particular event will have a very strong negative influence on another event in the corresponding column, a +10 means an event will have a very strong positive effect, and a zero indicates no probable impact. All degrees (i.e., numbers) of influence are potential choices—a continuum from −10 through zero to +10.

Table 11
Cross-Impact Matrix for Five Possible Educational Events[110]

No.	Events Effect Of	Probability	Estimated Year of Occurrence	Impacts Effect on Event No.				
				1	2	3	4	5
1	Laws requiring negotiation between school boards and teacher unions	.7	1978	—	10	4	3	1
2	All teachers in unions	.9	1976	8	—	6	8	4
3	Most students in unions	.3	2000	0	2	—	8	9
4	Voucher plan mandatory in half of states	.4	1980	6	8	0	—	10
5	20% in enrollment in "new schools"	.8	1980	-5	-7	6	10	—

Simulation Techniques

Social science research is relying more and more on simulation techniques to simplify the complex social relations involved in human social groups and societies. In this context, a simulation is a simplification and an approximation of some aspect of social reality. As a dress pattern is a static model of a real entity, so a simulation is a dynamic model of a social event. A simulation may take the form of a mechanical analog (such as a cockpit model for training pilots or astronauts); a mathematical analog (such as equations describing small group interactions); a metaphorical analog (such as "actors," "roles," and "stage" standing for "persons," "relationships," and "setting" or "environment"); and a game analog (such as *Monopoly*, which simulates competition in the real estate development market).

Simulation models depict the essential structure and dynamic interactions in the process leading to a future setting. Because many factors and interactions are usually involved, futurists often resort to computers to handle the complex models.

Simulations are useful to futurists as tools for:

1. Predicting the future results of current actions.

2. Testing several alternative futures.

3. Analyzing the effects of trade-offs.

4. Designing complex experiments.

5. Managing complex systems.

Systems Analysis

This is a futures research methodology particularly suited to making public policy decisions. A general definition for a system is "a defined collection of elements with their interconnections considered over a period of time."[111] Once the "collection of elements" and "their interconnections" have been defined, the system then can be analyzed. Analysis, in this context, "means that an entity can be resolved into its constituent elements and their relationships and then be examined again."[112]

If, for example, we consider a public school third-grade class as a system (a social system), this implies that a collection of elements is present, that these elements are somehow interconnected, and that the system can be observed in operation over time. These conditions do exist in our example of the third-grade class: the teacher, the students, the classroom, and the materials and artifacts in the classroom are the elements. These elements are interconnected, though the connections are sociological and psychological rather than physical. Furthermore, the class-as-system is goal-directed or purposeful and is dynamic or changing over time so that it can be analyzed in respect to changes toward or away from its goal(s) or purpose(s) and at various points in time. Each time this class-as-system is analyzed, not only are the changes with respect to the system's goal(s) revealed, but these data can also be used by any authorized and interested decision maker to intervene in, modify, or veer the system. In this example, such a decision maker might be within the system (the teacher or one or more students) or outside the system (the school principal or one or more parents).

Two of the most difficult aspects of systems analysis are defining the system and selecting and utilizing the appropriate techniques of analysis. Using the third-grade class example again, consider the difficulties of defining the system's goals, of setting the boundaries of the system, of describing sufficiently the human components of the system (the teacher and students), and of specifying the numerous interactions of the system [teacher-student(s) interactions, student(s)-student(s) interactions, and human-physical object interactions]. Also, consider the problems inherent in selecting and utilizing techniques for observing and recording changes in the system over time—of assessing what is happening in the classroom, what changes in interactions are occurring, what progress is being made toward component or system goals, what are the effects from internal or external interventions in the system.

Systems analysis has become a useful futures methodology in educational policy research. Among its uses as a source for educational decision makers are the following:

1. Analysis of basic issues involved in decisions relating to the funding and control of schools.

2. Descriptions of feasible alternative future educational systems and of the policy decisions that would tend to lead toward each.

3. Comparison of alternative means (e.g., instructional techniques) for aiming toward a set of goals (e.g., learning objectives).

4. Analysis of the dynamics of implementing a particular innovation, especially the anticipated interactions among advocates and opponents of the planned change.[113]

Consensus Methods

These techniques are used to derive knowledge on topics or problems that do not lend themselves to precise formulations or experiments, but which have been probed, in one way or another, by a number of practitioners and scholars who have become expert in one of these fields. Thus, what is sought is a consensus or modal tendency on a particular problem or issue among a group of experts.

One popular consensus method is the Delphi technique:

> Generally a Delphi exercise engages experts in an anonymous debate, their opinions being exchanged through an intermediary. Anonymity exists at two levels; not only are participants unknown to each other, but the individual responses are never attributed to particular respondents. In the first round of a typical Delphi study, the participants might be asked when a future event might take place. Their answers would be collated by the experimenters and fed back to them in a second round. The second-round questionnaire would seek justification of extreme views expressed in round one. The responses would again be collated by the experimenters and furnished to the participants in a third (and usually final) round. This questionnaire would ask that the experts reassess their previous positions in view of those taken by the other participants....

> The Delphi technique generally produces a narrowing of the initial spread of opinions and a shifting of the median as the questioning proceeds. If no consensus emerges, at least a crystallizing of the disparate positions usually becomes apparent.[114]

Perhaps the easiest way to understand the Delphi process is to see how it might be used by an educational futurist. In the case study presented here the scope of the questionnaire has been limited, as has the sample of "experts" querried. Since the process involves a sequence of *steps* and a number of *rounds*, our example will be described in these terms.

> Step 1 — The futurist determines the focus of the research in terms of topics and/or questions in education and also the future time frame (e.g., present to the year 2000) to be explored. At the same time, a decision needs to be made as to how the items for the Round 1 questionnaire are to be generated (e.g., from the literature, from a poll of experts, by the futurist researcher).

> Step 2 — The researcher derives and compiles a list of potential participants (i.e., experts) in the Delphi poll, including names, addresses, and telephone numbers. Each person on the list is contacted to secure his/her willingness to participate in the research and also to elicit suggestions of other experts who might be included in the Delphi study. Now is an appropriate juncture to decide how to send questionnaires to the participants and receive their feedback for each of the three to five Delphi rounds. The typical mode is first-class mail, but the telephone or telephone plus computer are also used in these polls.

By this point in the process, the participant population is ready to receive the Round 1 questionnaire by some mode of communication, and the format and substance of the questionnaire have been formalized. On pages 51-52 is a sample questionnaire that was used in Round 1, with a small group of 20 "experts" — graduate students in a course on social and educational futures.

Round 1 — In this round, participants receive, complete, and return the questionnaire. The researcher tabulates and compile the results of Round 1, and then prepares the material to be sent out in Round 2. On page 53 are the results of our Round 1 example.

Delphi Questionaire
Round 1

This questionnaire is the first (Round 1) in a series of three rounds intended to gain relative consensus amoung participants in the survey. For each of the 10 items, you are asked for two responses: (1) when the event or situation will occur, and (2) how desirable for public education the event or situation will be. Use only the numbers for future time ranges and degrees of desirability.

Future Time Ranges	Degrees of Desirability
1 = 1985 - 1989	1 = Highly Desirable
2 = 1990 - 1994	2 = Somewhat Desirable
3 = 1995 - 1999	3 = Uncertain
4 = 2000 - 2009	4 = Somewhat Undesirable
5 = 2010 - 2019	5 = Highly Undesirable

Delphi Questionnaire

Round 1

Future Time Range

Degree of Desirability

_____ 1. All funding for public education will come from state and federal sources; none from local school district funds. _____

_____ 2. Collective bargaining by teacher unions (ADT or NEA) will be universal in all 50 states. _____

_____ 3. Collective bargaining by principals and assistant principals will be universal in all 50 states. _____

_____ 4. Collective bargaining by public education personnel will be done at the state level only; no longer will bargaining occur by school district. _____

_____ 5. Local school boards for each district in a state will be abolished; each state will be a single school district (as in Hawaii today). _____

_____ 6. School buildings will be used an average of 12 hours per day, for 300 days per year (currently the numbers are 6 and 185). _____

_____ 7. Various types of computers (including microcomputers) will "teach" and "monitor" learning for 10-15 hours per school week (of a total 25-30 hours in a school week). _____

_____ 8. Approximately 25 percent of homes with school-age children will have electronic learning systems (with two to four terminals per system), and parents will contract with school officials for 25-50 percent of an academic year curriculum to occur at home. _____

_____ 9. Some form of voucher system or tax credit for tuition will give parents and students choices of schools from among a variety of public, private (nonprofit), proprietary (profit-making), and parochial schools. _____

_____ 10. Fewer teachers will be paid higher salaries to develop curricula (50 percent of time), to tutor individuals (25 percent of time), to lead/monitor small groups of 5-15 students (15 percent of time), and to give lecture/demonstrations (10 percent of time). _____

Delphi Questionnaire

Round 1 – Results

Future Time Range			**Degree of Desirability**

4 (3.6)* 1. All funding for public education will come from state and federal sources; none from local school district funds. 4 (3.7)*

3 (2.7) 2. Collective bargaining by teacher unions (ADT or NEA) will be universal in all 50 states. 3 (3.1)

3 (3.2) 3. Collective bargaining by principals and assistant principals will be universal in all 50 states. 3 (3.0)

3 (3.5) 4. Collective bargaining by public education personnel will be done at the state level only; no longer will bargaining occur by school district. 4 (3.6)

4 (4.2) 5. Local school boards for each district in a state will be abolished; each state will be a single school district (as in Hawaii today). 4 (3.9)

2 (2.5) 6. School buildings will be used an average of 12 hours per day, for 300 days per year (currently the numbers are 6 and 185). 2 (2.4)

2 (2.5) 7. Various types of computers (including microcomputers) will "teach" and "monitor" learning for 10-15 hours per school week (of a total 25-30 hours in a school week). 3 (2.7)

3 (3.4) 8. Approximately 25 percent of homes with school-age children will have electronic learning systems (with two to four terminals per system), and parents will contract with school officials for 25-50 percent of an academic year curriculum to occur at home. 3 (2.7)

2 (1.7) 9. Some form of voucher system or tax credit for tuition will give parents and students choices of schools from among a variety of public, private (nonprofit), proprietary (profit-making), and parochial schools. 3 (2.7)

3 (3.0) 10. Fewer teachers will be paid higher salaries to develop curricula (50 percent of time), to tutor individuals (25 percent of time), to lead/monitor small groups of 5-15 students (15 percent of time), and to give lecture/demonstrations (10 percent of time). 2 (2.3)

*The number in parentheses is the mean score, where the number of participants is 20.

One can interpret the above results for Round 1 in the following manner. The number before the parenthesis in the left column (headed "Future Time Range") refers to the numbers in front of the five time ranges:

Future Time Ranges

1 = 1985 - 1989
2 = 1990 - 1994
3 = 1995 - 1999
4 = 2000 - 2009
5 = 2010 - 2019

The number before the parenthesis in the right column refer to "Degrees of Desirability":

Degrees of Desirability

1 = Highly Desirable
2 = Somewhat Desirable
3 = Uncertain
4 = Somewhat Undesirable
5 = Highly Undesirable

Thus, for item (i.e., forecast) 1 on the Round 1 Delphi Questionnaire—concerning sources of funding for public education—the 20 Delphi respondents' mean for "Future Time Range" was 3.6, which was converted to a "4" or "2000 – 2009." For the same item, the mean on "Degrees of Desirability" was 3.7, converted to a "4" or "Somewhat Undesirable."

Other generalizations that can be made from Round 1 results are:

1. That item 9 will occur soonest.

2. That the order of occurrence for the 10 items is: 9, 6, 7, 2, 10, 3, 8, 4, 1, 5.

3. That the most desirable event is 10; while the least desirable occurrence is item 1.

4. That those desirable events that will occur soonest are 9 and 6.

Another way of computing and displaying the Round 1 results is by median score and interquartile range. This procedure is depicted in Figures 9 and 10.

Visualized in this way, certain characteristics of the poll results are readily visible. For example, only one event falls clearly in the 1985-89 range—item 9. Or looking at "Degrees of Desirability," the 10 events seem to cluster into three groups: Desirable—items 6 through 10; Undesirable—items 4 and 5; and Uncertain—items 1, 2, and 3.

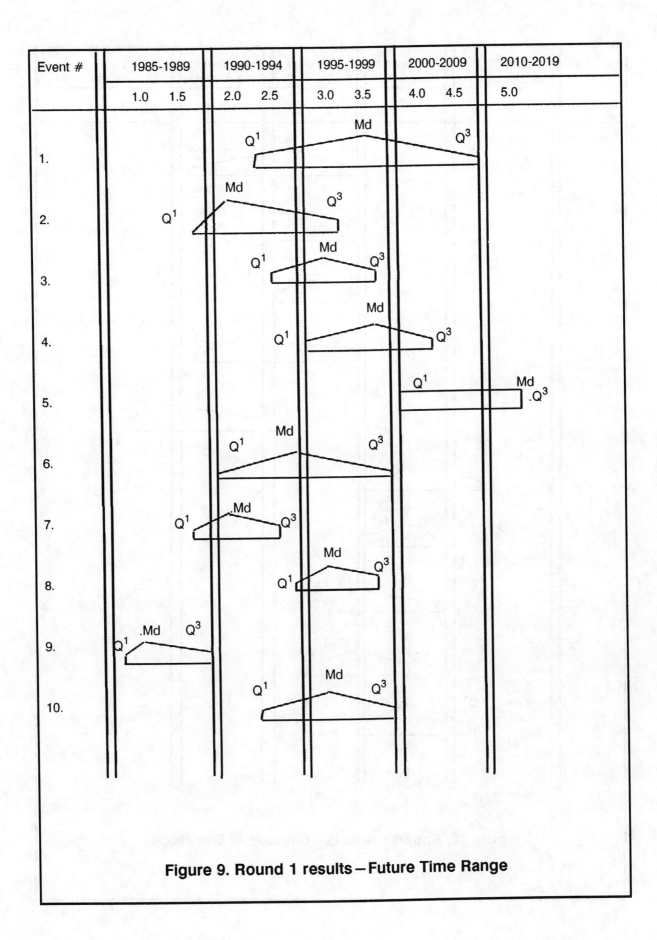

Figure 9. Round 1 results – Future Time Range

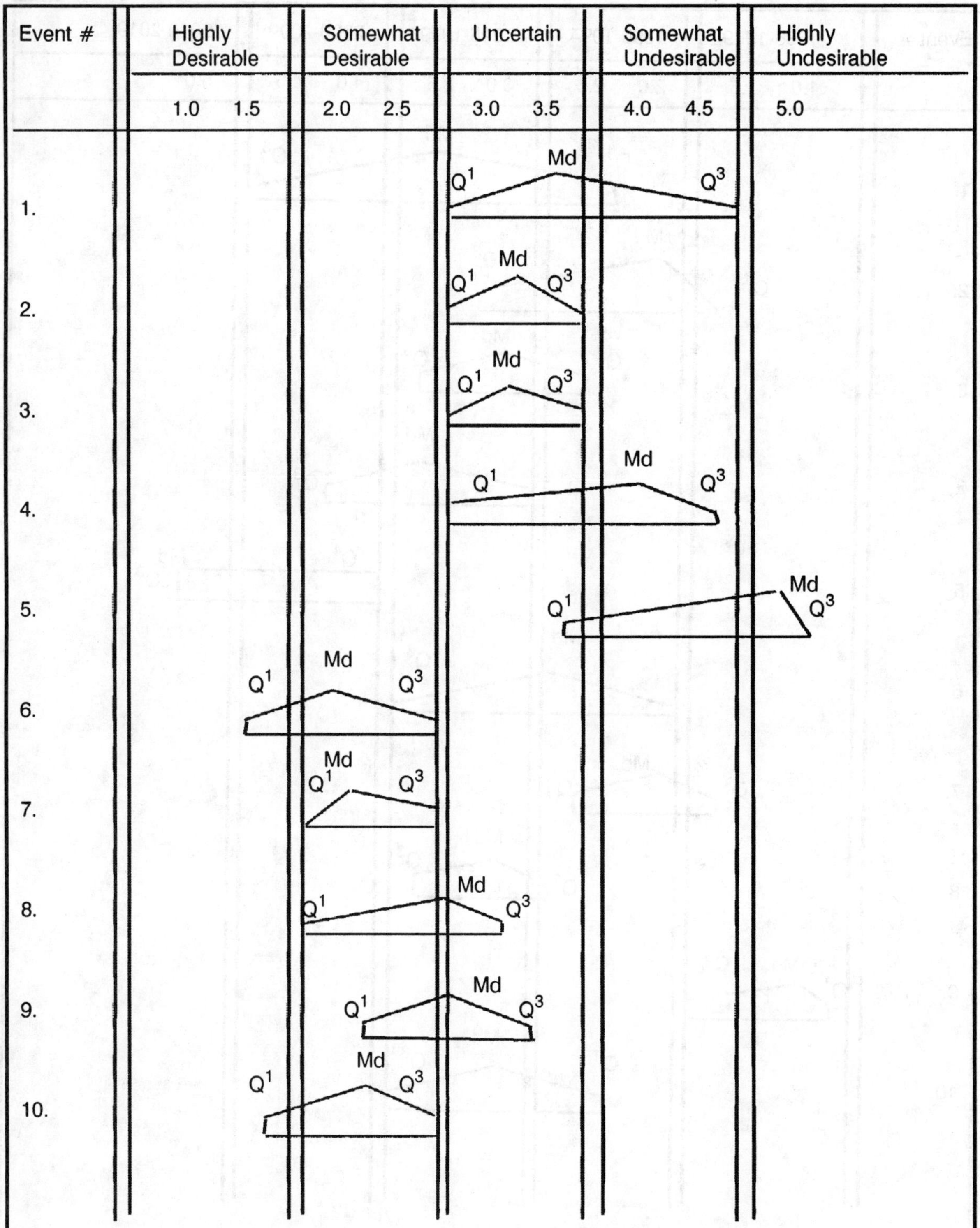

Figure 10. Round 1 results—Degrees of Desirability

Round 2—The questionnaire for this round is the same as that used in Round 1, except that there are two additional items included for Round 2. The first of these is a summary of the results of Round 1, and the second is a statement of special directions for the new round:

In Round 2, if you choose a "Future Time Range" or a "Degree of Desirability" *that is different from the mean category* shown in the enclosed results of Round 1, you must *also supply a succinct statement of justification for your choice.*

For example, on questionnaire item 1, if you select any time range other than 2000-2009, you need to write out a cryptic justification for your choice. The same would be true if you selected a degree of desirability (again for item 1) other than "Somewhat Undesirable." Thus, it is possible but not likely that you would have to write as many as 20 justifications.

For your convenience, a "Justifications Form" is attached to your Round 2 Questionnaire to be filled out only for appropriate items.

The Delphi participant receives in addition to the above set of directions a blank questionnaire to which is stapled a "Justifications Form" (see page 59) and the results of Round 1 (as summarized on page 53). Round 2 feedback to the Delphi director includes a completed questionnaire with attached justifications (if any). Again the researcher compiles and computes results as in the first round, but in addition he/she summarizes the anecdotal justifications for "deviant" choices on questionnaire items. In our illustrative case, the Round 2 results (including justifications) are shown on the following pages.

Delphi Questionnaire

Round 2 — Results

Future Time Range		**Degree of Desirability**
4 (3.6)^{nc}	1. All funding for public education will come from state and federal sources; none from local school district funds.	4 (3.7)^{nc}
3 (2.7)^{nc}	2. Collective bargaining by teacher unions (ADT or NEA) will be universal in all 50 states.	3 (3.1)^{nc}
3 (3.2)^{nc}	3. Collective bargaining by principals and assistant principals will be universal in all 50 states.	3 (3.0)^{nc}
3 (3.5)^{nc}	4. Collective bargaining by public education personnel will be done at the state level only; no longer will bargaining occur by school district.	4 (3.6)^{nc}
4 (4.2)^{nc}	5. Local school boards for each district in a state will be abolished; each state will be a single school district (as in Hawaii today).	4 (3.9)^{nc}
2 (2.2)	6. School buildings will be used an average of 12 hours per day, for 300 days per year (currently the numbers are 6 and 185).	2 (2.1)
2 (2.5)^{nc}	7. Various types of computers (including microcomputers) will "teach" and "monitor" learning for 10-15 hours per school week (of a total 25-30 hours in a school week).	2 (2.4)
3 (3.4)^{nc}	8. Approximately 25 percent of homes with school-age children will have electronic learning systems (with two to four terminals per system), and parents will contract with school officials for 25-50 percent of an academic year curriculum to occur at home.	3 (2.7)^{nc}
1 (1.4)	9. Some form of voucher system or tax credit for tuition will give parents and students choices of schools from among a variety of public, private (nonprofit), proprietary (profit-making), and parochial schools.	2 (2.4)
3 (3.0)^{nc}	10. Fewer teachers will be paid higher salaries to develop curricula (50 percent of time), to tutor individuals (25 percent of time), to lead/monitor small groups of 5-15 students (15 percent of time), and to give lecture/demonstrations (10 percent of time).	2 (2.3)^{nc}

^{nc} = no change from Round 1.

```
┌─────────────────────────────────────────────────────────────────────┐
│                      Delphi Questionnaire                            │
│                                                                     │
│                 Round 2 — Justifications Form                       │
│                                                                     │
│  Item        Future Time Range            Degree of Desirability    │
│                                                                     │
│  1.    Equity laws and court cases will make   Teachers need higher salaries and greater │
│        this happen sooner.                     bargaining power.    │
│                                                                     │
│  2.    _____                              _____           │
│                                                                     │
│  3.    _____                              _____           │
│                                                                     │
│  4.    _____                              _____           │
│                                                                     │
│  5.    Due to citizen opposition this will never  _____        │
│        happen.                                                      │
│                                                                     │
│  6.    Energy crisis will bring this about sooner.  Highly desirable to use building more. │
│                                                                     │
│  7.    _____                              Highly desirable to save labor costs. │
│                                                                     │
│  8.    _____                              _____           │
│                                                                     │
│  9.    Many pressure groups oppose this and    Will make public schools only for the │
│        will delay it.                          poor and for minority ethnics. │
│                                                                     │
│  10.   _____                              _____           │
└─────────────────────────────────────────────────────────────────────┘
```

Looking at the Round 2 results, the first evident conclusion is that there were few changes from the previous round. While five mean scores changed (counting both columns), there were only three category shifts, affecting just two items — 7 (Desirability only) and 9 (Range and Desirability). Note that on the justifications form, respondents made statements on five items.

Round 3 — In this round, the Delphi respondents again receive the Round 1 questionnaire with attached blank justifications form. They also receive the Round 2 results; in addition, they are sent a compilation of justifications from the second round forms. As in Round 2, participants are given special directions about when statements of justification are required.

After all Round 3 materials have been logged in by the Delphi researcher, results and justifications are once again summarized. The Round 3 results and a justifications form compilation are prepared for the Round 4 mailing. These forms are not presented again here due to considerable redundancy with Round 2.

Round 4 — This is the final round in our sample Delphi exercise. Thus, the participants are asked only to complete the questionnaire a last time without bothering about justifications for their choices. Of course it is expected they will take into consideration the Round 3 justifications before making their final decisions.

The final poll results are presented with actual time ranges and statements of desirability.

Delphi Questionnaire

Final Results

Future Time Range			Degree of Desirability
2000-2009	1.	All funding for public education will come from state and federal sources; none from local school district funds.	Somewhat Undesirable
1995-1999	2.	Collective bargaining by teacher unions (ADT or NEA) will be universal in all 50 states.	Uncertain
1995-1999	3.	Collective bargaining by principals and assistant principals will be universal in all 50 states.	Uncertain
1995-1999	4.	Collective bargaining by public education personnel will be done at the state level only; no longer will bargaining occur by school district.	Somewhat Undesirable
2000-2009	5.	Local school boards for each district in a state will be abolished; each state will be a single school district (as in Hawaii today).	Somewhat Undesirable
1990-1994	6.	School buildings will be used an average of 12 hours per day, for 300 days per year (currently the numbers are 6 and 185).	Highly Desirable
1990-1994	7.	Various types of computers (including microcomputers) will "teach" and "monitor" learning for 10-15 hours per school week (of a total 25-30 hours in a school week).	Somewhat Desirable
1995-1999	8.	Approximately 25 percent of homes with school-age children will have electronic learning systems (with two to four terminals per system), and parents will contract with school officials for 25-50 percent of an academic year curriculum to occur at home.	Uncertain
1985-1989	9.	Some form of voucher system or tax credit for tuition will give parents and students choices of schools from among a variety of public, private (nonprofit), proprietary (profit-making), and parochial schools.	Somehwat Desirable
1995-1999	10.	Fewer teachers will be paid higher salaries to develop curricula (50 percent of time), to tutor individuals (25 percent of time), to lead/monitor small groups of 5-15 students (15 percent of time), and to give lecture/demonstrations (10 percent of time).	Somewhat Desirable

These eight futures research methodologies or forecasting skills can provide us with useful hunches, clues, or probabilities about the future, or, more accurately, about possible or probable alternative futures. But they cannot provide us with predictability or certainty concerning future events. The future is still an open system that remains amenable to human decisions and interventions.

The many reasons why forecasts go wrong should be kept in mind when studying futurists' forecasts:

1. Unforeseeable historical accidents may occur.

2. A forecast may itself spur decisions and interventions that invalidate the forecast.

3. The use of invalid comparisons of analogies between past and future situations may invalidate the forecast.

4. The futurist may misinterpret cause-and-effect relationships.

5. A forecaster may allow his/her desires to cloud plausibility.

6. The investigator may have used unreliable information or lacked pertinent data.

7. A futurist may lack imagination and/or nerve.

8. Incorrect calculations or varieties of overcompensation may occur.

9. The forecaster may become preoccupied with a single pattern and/or omit pertinent developments.

4. THE FUTURE IN THE CURRICULUM

Our only choice with respect to the study of the future

> is between being completely surprised by the future and therefore wholly subject to the control of external forces or, alternatively, having some basis of knowledge about what is possible so that [we] can attempt to shape the future in accordance with [our] own desires and values.[115]

To study the future is a commitment to freedom, to the use of our margin of freedom in the face of all the forces that would predetermine our futures. To study the future is a commitment to the worth and survival of the human species, to the link between the generations—young, old, and yet to be born.

For teachers and students, reasons for studying the future are at the same time alike and different. Both teachers and students are curious and full of wonder; they want to know and shape their personal and mutual futures; they are seekers, probing the multiple realities of their universe; and they value a just and joyous survival of their common species. Yet their justifications and motivations for studying the future differ.

Teachers pursue and benefit from futures study for several reasons. First, the topic is inherently relevant to their clients because children and youth will spend three-fourths to four-fifths of their lives in the future. Second, as Richard Bach observed in his best seller, *Illusions*, "You teach best what you most need to learn."[116] Third, there is no dearth of fascinating and appealing topics and materials. Finally, futures study can fit into and draw on virtually every subject area in the curriculum, at any and all grade levels; it is a ubiquitous, multidisciplinary subject.

Reasons for having students study the future are numerous and varied, but probably the most important justification is to help them improve their skills in making wise decisions, as individuals and as citizens. Other reasons are:[117]

1. To acclimate them to life in a changing world.

2. To provide them with frameworks for cooperation, reconciliation, and conflict management.

3. To foster creativity.

4. To stimulate learning as both a pleasant and useful process.

5. To help them develop appealing and worthwhile images of the future as well as personal philosophies of life.

6. To help them identify dangers and opportunities.

7. To enable them to see the present.

8. To influence their degree of choice.

Curriculum Decisions

Once a social studies teacher decides to have his/her students study the future, the question becomes where to include what in the curriculum. Ready responses are anywhere and everywhere, anything and everything, but these are not particularly useful to the teacher. Therefore, let us look at some more practical possibilities.

Classroom teachers would do well to begin planning by consulting with other teachers in their own school or district, as well as with local futurists or teachers of futures courses at nearby colleges or universities. Next, every teacher should heed these guidelines provided by Draper Kauffman:[118]

1. Begin with the student's own personal image of the future....

2. Relate *all* subject matter to the future needs of the students.

3. Apportion space in the [futures] curriculum to different subjects....

4. Explain the rationale for the curriculum choices to students, [parents, and others].

5. Allow the flexibility to accommodate differences in interests, ability, and future plans [of the student].

6. Present content in an interdisciplinary manner, emphasizing the underlying similarities of all living and social systems.

7. Organize the learning environment to stimulate creativity, self-motivated learning, and self-discovery.

8. Emphasize skills over knowledge, helping students learn 'sciencing' as well as science, forecasting as well as forecasts—in short, thinking as well as facts.

Futures Categories

One source for deriving possible content for futures courses at any grade level is a list of futures categories. The teacher might choose a number of categories (one or two per unit, or three or four per semester course, or six to eight per academic year course) and topics (maybe five or six per category) and use them to build a unit or course. A suggested list follows.

Communication

1. Automated services (banking, supermarkets)
2. Computers (micro-, networks, intelligence)
3. Human/machine interactions
4. Picturephone and portable telephones
5. Television (three-dimensional, 100-channel, two-way broadcasts, cable)
6. Space satellite stations (planetwide networks)
7. Information processing
8. Extraterrestrial intelligence and communication

Energy and Other Natural Resources

1. Pollution
2. Fossil fuels (oil, coal, gas, geothermal)
3. Solar energy
4. Synthetic fuels
5. Fuel cells (lead-acid battery)
6. Nuclear energy (fission, breeder, fusion)
7. Land
8. Air
9. Water
10. Endangered species (flora and fauna)
11. Environmental protection policies and practices
12. Weather and climate modification

Family Life

1. Fertility control (contraceptives, abortion, family planning)
2. Women's liberation and occupations
3. Sex, courtship, and marriage patterns
4. Size of family and household
5. Genetic engineering (sex of fetus, cloning)

Food and Agriculture

1. Arable land
2. Use of fertilizers
3. Crop yields
4. Droughts and famines
5. Ocean farming
6. Malnutrition and starvation
7. Diet (babies, calories, proteins)

Health

1. Organ transplant and prosthetic devices
2. Cancer and other terminal diseases
3. Pharmacology (drugs)
4. Infant mortality and problems of aging
5. Euthanasia (extraordinary life support, brain death)
6. National health systems (insurance, health care delivery)
7. Cryogenics
8. Mind altering (hallucinogens, "smart pills")
9. Epidemics (immunization and sanitation)
10. Drug addiction and alcoholism
11. Mental health

Community and Habitat

1. Home robots
2. New towns and cities
3. Urbanization (megalopolises, inner-city life)
4. House architecture and construction (building materials, designs, rent, financing ownership, "condomania," second homes)
5. Intentional communities (rural and urban communes, voluntary simplicity)
6. Synthetic and natural environments (environmental engineering)
7. Demography (population mobility and stability, community size)
8. Open space (parks, recreation)
9. Unusual habitats (oceans, underground)

Values, Attitudes, and Lifestyles

1. Country-cultural lifestyles
2. Social pathologies (alienation, helplessness, boredom, future shock)
3. "New age" consciousness
4. Mysticism
5. ESP and paranormal phenomena
6. Emergent and traditional values
7. Institutional work and life (bureaucracy, standardization, specialization, loss of freedom and efficacy)
8. Materialist vs. nonmaterialist values, philosophies, and lifestyles

9. Privacy and confidentiality
10. Information overload, confusion, incapacitation
11. Racism and sexism
12. Credentialism and meritocracy
13. New religions, changing older religions

Transportation

1. Nonfossil fuel automobile and airplane engines
2. Air traffic control and safety of planes
3. Mass transportation
4. Walking and bicycling
5. Oil tankers and merchant marine fleets
6. Urban traffic flows and patterns
7. Urban carbon dioxide/monoxide pollution
8. Speed and convenience
9. Space exploration and colonization

Work and Leisure

1. Overconsumption and superabundance
2. New avocations and leisure pursuits
3. Unemployment and underemployment
4. Craft and quality (workmanship and productivity)
5. Poverty, guaranteed income, negative income tax
6. Collective bargaining issues (profit sharing, cost of living indexing, vacation time, shared corporate governance)
7. Consumer issues (dangerous products, quality, damaged goods, pricing practices)
8. Occupations (in production of goods, services, knowledge, and technology; new kinds of job such as geriatric nurse or computer security guard or exobiologist)

Government and Economics

1. Inflation and unemployment
2. Recession and depression
3. Crime and violence
4. Police powers such as surveillance
5. Metropolitan and regional government
6. Local, state, and federal tax structures
7. Welfare and social services
8. Control of technology
9. Financing research and development
10. Authoritarianism
11. Citizen dissent and efficacy; participation
12. Types of decision-making formats and processes
13. Centralization of power
14. Planning and management of social change
15. Ideologies
16. New scarcities and limits to growth (resource economics, scaling down, steady-state economy)
17. Profit, pricing, productivity, capital investment, interest rates, money supply

International Affairs

1. The rich and poor nations (redistribution of wealth, commodity pricing, balance of payments, trade agreements, power blocs)
2. Regulating the transnational corporations (control of trade, taxation)

3. "Ugly American" stereotype, problems of cross-cultural living, multilingualism, world religions
4. United Nations and prospects for world federalism and world law
5. Regulating use of oceans, air, space
6. Terror and nuclear blackmail, "limited" war, thermonuclear war, civil war
7. International monetary system, world bank, development loans
8. Urbanization (urban growth and squalor)
9. Poverty, famine, drought, and starvation; relief for natural disasters
10. Production and sale of military weapons, arms limitation treaties, storage of long-lived nuclear energy waste products, size of military establishments
11. Rising expectations and demonstration effects
12. International elites (powerful, wealthy, famous persons)

Education

1. New careers (home educator, industrial educator, gerontologist)
2. Affective and experiential education
3. Enrollments (private and public schools, K-12 and college-university)
4. Education of the handicapped
5. Problems of schools as institutions (depersonalization, bureaucracy, alienation)
6. Deschooling schemes and voucher plans
7. Teacher unionism
8. Legal rights of students and teachers
9. Pre-primary education (ages 1 to 5)
10. Instructional technologies ("hardware" and "software")
11. Human relations and interpersonal skill training
12. Financing schools, colleges and universities, economics of equal educational opportunity
13. School-as-community, social system, school and society
14. Problems of "under-" and "over-education"
15. Stages of lifelong education
16. Centralization of authority and decentralization and community control
17. Global and future studies

Learning Objectives for a Futures-Oriented Curriculum[119]

A second list might also prove useful. This one suggests categories and types of *skills* that could be emphasized in a study of the future.

Access to Information

1. Reading
2. Listening and seeing
3. Direct experiment
4. Libraries and reference books
5. Computerized data retrieval
6. Data from newspapers, businesses, government agencies, etc.
7. Asking experts
8. Judging reliability
9. Managing information overload

Thinking Clearly

1. Semantics
2. Propaganda and common fallacies
3. Values clarification
4. Deductive logic

5. Mathematics
6. Analytical problem solving
7. Scientific method
8. Probability and statistics
9. Computer programming
10. General systems
11. Creative problem solving
12. Forecasting and prediction

Communicating Effectively

1. Speaking informally
2. Public speaking
3. Voice and body language
4. Cultural barriers to communication
5. Formal and informal writing
6. Grammar, syntax, and style
7. Drawing, sketching, still photography, film making, etc.
8. Graphic design and layout
9. Outlines, flow charts, charts, tables, and graphs
10. Organization and editing
11. Handwriting, typing, dictating

Understanding the Environment

1. Astronomy, physics, and chemistry
2. Geology and physical geography
3. Biology, ecology, and ethology
4. Genetics, evolution, and population dynamics
5. Fundamentals of modern technology
6. Applied mechanics, optics, and electronics

Understanding People and Society

1. Human evolution
2. Human physiology
3. Linguistics
4. Cultural anthropology (including history and the humanities)
5. Psychology and social psychology
6. Racism, ethnicity, and xenophobia
7. Government and law (especially American constitutional law)
8. Economics and economic philosophy
9. Changing occupational patterns
10. Education and employment
11. Issues in human survival
12. Prospects for humans

Personal Competence

1. Physical grace and coordination
2. Survival training and self-defense
3. Safety, hygiene, nutrition, and sex education
4. Consumer education and personal finance
5. Creative and performing arts
6. Basic interpersonal skills
7. Small group dynamics

8. Management and administration
9. Effective citizen participation
10. Knowledge of best personal learning styles and strategies
11. Mnemonics and other learning aids
12. Biofeedback, meditation, mood control
13. Self-knowledge and self-motivation

Focus for a Futures Curriculum

Next is a list of values, attitudes, behaviors, and skills that a teacher might use as focuses for a futures curriculum.[120]

Values and Attitudes

1. Less fear of the unknown and a greater trust and respect for diversity of people and lifestyles will predominate.

2. A willingness to explore new patterns of interaction and flexibility rather than rigidity will characterize human behavior.

3. A high value on creativity as an essentiality for individual and collective survival and self-actualization will be realized.

4. An emphais on the quality of life rather than the quantity of material possessions will predominate.

5. A renewed social commitment to the value of human life will be operationalized.

6. A renewed respect for nature, as opposed to current beliefs that nature is here only for human use, and a biosphere perspective will prevail.

7. Global loyalty rather than competitive nationalism will guide the interaction of populations in different geographic areas.

8. A willingness to share the world's resources equally will be achieved.

9. A reintegration of human intellect, feelings, and body, and a greater trust in sensory and emotional experience will be manifested in societal attitudes.

10. A greater emphasis on cooperation rather than competition will characterize the relations between individuals and groups.

11. A belief in the unlimited potentiality of people, both individually and collectively, will be evidenced in the support individuals receive from their institutions.

12. A commitment to achieve and maintain a balance between individual actions and the common good will characterize individual and government decision-making.

13. A belief in human ability to collaboratively create and maintain a humanistic, dynamic, equilibrium society will serve as a mission shared by all.

14. Authority will derive from competence and knowledge rather than from role and power.

15. Equal respect for manual, intellectual, and aesthetic endeavors will be manifested by equal respect and equality in the distribution of resources.

16. Individuals will delight in the multiple choices available at any decision point.

Behaviors

1. Individuals will exhibit a high tolerance for ambiguity and be relaxed when confronted with uncertainty, and will have the emotional ability to struggle with problems for which there are not easy and specific answers.

2. When in problem-solving and planning situations, people will initiate an automatic searching for all possible alternatives and options, anticipate contingencies, and predict long-range as well as short-range effects.

3. Persons will utilize a variety of holistic analytical techniques for problem solving. Future people can no longer rely on precedent, linear forecasting, analogy, and extrapolation—all such methods assume a static world rather than a dynamic world.

4. Conceptualization will be characterized by an emphasis on the interrelatedness of global parts-- that is, the comprehension of complex wholes and the understanding of specific parts within the context of the complex whole.

5. Cognitive and affective processes that extend human ability to conceptualize globally and in extensive time frames must be developed.

6. Groups will approach all decision-making activity committed to a collaborative process of consensual validation that seeks alternatives to win-lose models.

7. Individuals and groups will engage in a continuing process of self-renewal and will initiate actions that insure self-renewal for all.

8. It will be expected that processes be initiated and sustained for value clarification for individuals and groups.

9. Most actions will be characterized by altruistic behavior.

10. Most interaction will be characterized by cooperative rather than competitive behavior.

11. Interpersonal communications and interaction will be formed and severed rapidly.

12. Self- and group discipline will be initiated to control the use of resources.

13. Sharing will be commonplace.

14. Individuals will be self-reliant and group-reliant and be able to shift from one to another as necessary.

15. Persons will manage self-change and be able to participate in the management of group change.

16. Collaboration with others will be an expected behavior.

17. Authentic behavior that integrates intellect, feelings, and body will be exhibited at all times.

18. Persons will individually and collectively act for what is believed to be desirable.

19. The ability to communicate with a variety of individuals will be essential.

20. The initiation of acts that will further one's self-actualization will be a continuous process.

21. Risk-taking behavior will not be avoided.

Skills

1. Information processing skills will be essential—especially the ability to store, retrieve, sort, and relate pertinent information to specific needs.

2. General and social systems analysis techniques will be required to better understand the complexity of various structures and to better perceive the reciprocity, connections, and interdependencies between and within systems.

3. Individual and group planning techniques will be needed so that individuals and groups can make better proactive decisions.

4. Value clarification techniques will need to be used extensively to clarify purposes and implicit values among alternative courses of action.

5. Individuals will need independent learning and unlearning techniques for their continuous growth and development.

6. Individual and group reinforcement techniques will be utilized to provide interpersonal support for individual and group growth and development.

7. Systems dynamics analysis and planning techniques will be widely used to understand the long-range consequences of current decisions.

8. A variety of communications techniques will be needed to enhance understanding between diverse individuals and groups.

9. Extensive linguistic ability in a variety of languages will be required to facilitate the development of global community and a respect for cultural diversity.

10. Most persons will need skill in a variety of manual skills to aid in the preservation and recycling of finite sources and to facilitate comprehensive personal development.

11. Forecasting skills will be needed to anticipate short-range and long-range consequences of proposed actions.

12. Counseling and group dynamics techniques are needed to aid others in their process of development and to increase effective communications in groups.

13. Each person will be able to use a variety of conceptual frameworks.

14. Aesthetic skills for personal expression and the development of new images will be essential for persons to fully self-actualize and for society to rise to new levels of synergy.

15. Skill in conflict management will be needed to aid communications, planning, and decision-making activities among diverse individuals and groups.

16. People will need techniques and processes to free sensory and emotional experience for full personal development.

A National Council for the Social Studies volume suggested another set of futures goals. The authors state that futures education should:[121]

1. Attempt to help students understand the concept of alternative futures.

2. Help the student understand the concept of change.

3. Promote an understanding of the possible modifications in human behavior necessary for the future.

4. Promote a holistic view of the natural and social worlds.

5. Promote an understanding of important societal trends and their implications.

6. Promote an understanding of the relationships between values and the future.

7. Promote an understanding of the ideas of major futurists and the methods of futurism.

8. Promote an understanding of the relationships between past, present, and future.

9. Promote a variety of additional perspectives and inquiry strategies.

10. Promote the general improvement of basic research and communications skills.

Finally, the National Academy of Science surveyed business leaders in order to determine the types of skills they would like to see in high school graduates. A large majority of those responding to the survey want high school graduates who are able to:[122]

1. Identify problems.

2. Evaluate alternative solutions, considering their costs and benefits.

3. Make logical decisions.

4. Distinguish fact from opinion.

5. Use established rules and facts to respond to unexpected situations.

6. Develop new ways of addressing persistent problems.

7. Determine what resources are needed to achieve work objectives.

8. Understand the purpose of written material.

9. Check the accuracy of information and evaluate the worth and objectivity of sources.

10. Interpret quantitative information such as that presented in tables, charts, and graphs.

Organizing the Futures Unit or Course

There are many unit/course schemes that teachers can use in organizing instruction on the topic of future studies. Several of these follow.

1. One approach that some teachers prefer because of the inherent appeal of the literature is to use science fiction short stories and books. In *Grokking the Future*, the authors propose a list of key topics and questions to use in dealing with any science fiction work:[123]

   a. Economic: What is considered wealth in this society? Who produces and who consumes products?

b. Political: How is order kept in the society? Who has the power? What allowance is made for the deviant or nonconformist? What sort of leader is considered "good"? What role does the military play? What would pose the greatest threat to the society? Why? What is the author's conception of man: Is man basically good? Bad? Trustworthy?

c. Social: What classes exist? How does one gain and lose status? Is status ascribed or achieved? In other words, does one gain status by birth or can one work his way up? How difficult is it to move from one class to another? What is the place of the family?

d. Religious: What religious beliefs prevail? What is the role of a supernatural being? How is the religion organized? Who holds the most religious power in the society?

e. Artistic: Is any allowance made for artistic and aesthetic expression? What kinds of art, music, literature, if any, exist in society? What role does the government play in controlling artistic and aesthetic expression?

f. Other Cultures: How does the society view other societies? Suspiciously?

g. General: How would you like living in this particular society? What would you find most distastful about it? What would you find most enjoyable about it? If you could change one thing in the society, what would you change and why? What would pose the greatest threat to the society? Why? To what extent do you see present-day American society in the story? What would have to specifically happen for American society to become like the story? How might this be prevented?

2. A "star-shaped" set of interactions among key topics (Figure 11) was used by Judith Hellfach in her teacher's guide to a four-booklet future course.

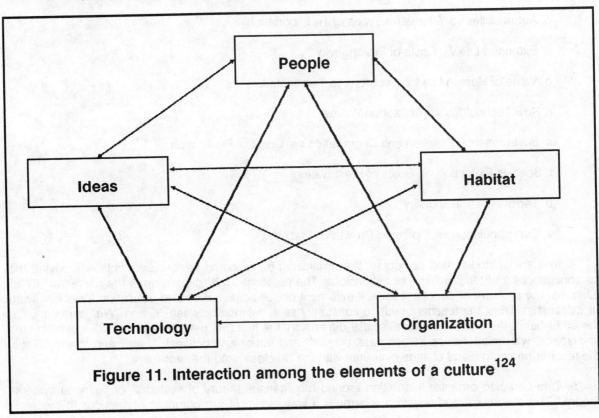

Figure 11. Interaction among the elements of a culture[124]

3. Edward Cornish, identified 22 "critical choices" he felt will be crucial to societies in the future:[125]

    a. Modern Societal Complexity vs. Participant Democracy

    b. Scale of Industrial Society vs. Human Needs for Community and Comradeship

    c. Worldwide "Free Trade" vs. Protectionism

    d. Social Cohesiveness vs. Plurality of Minority Cultures

    e. Nuclear Energy vs. Solar Energy, Conservation, and Shortages

    f. Humane and Preventive Criminology vs. Increased Crime Rate

    g. Representative Democracy vs. Instantaneous Electronic Direct Democracy

    h. Self-Realization vs. Family Nurturance

    i. National Security and War vs. Mutual Common Security and Conflict Management

    j. Free Migration vs. Restrictive Immigration Policies

    k. Poverty vs. Minimum Standard of Living

    l. Credentialing of Occupations vs. Employee "Risk" and Evaluation of Skills

    m. Rich (North) Nations vs. Poor (South) Nations

    n. Common Resources vs. Nationalization of Resources (e.g., Oceans)

    o. Automobiles vs. Alternative Types of Transportation

    p. Extended Life vs. Costs of Prolongevity

    q. Value of Human Life vs. Decisions to Terminate Life

    r. New Technology vs. Impact on Values

    s. Environmental Pollution and Degradation vs. Costs of Purification

    t. Species Extinction vs. Costs of Preservation

    u. Terrorism vs. Tranquility

    v. Overpopulation vs. Optimum Growth or Stability

4. In a social studies unit or course, the organizing frame could be four concepts embodying the personal/social and temporal/spatial dimensions. The personal/social dimension is the pervasive "I/We" dilemma, the problem of education for self-fulfillment or self-actualization *and* education for social living or citizenship. Thus, the teacher needs to constantly seek balance between "I" and "We" concerns. On the other hand, there is the temporal/spatial dimension, the fact that persons and societies exist in time and space, with relationships across past, present, and future and between "here" and "there." Thus, the teacher needs to blend change over time with the "in-close" and the "out-there."

5. One can also organize instruction around the "general theory of systems" or "general systems theory." This theoretical and research scheme is a way of simplifying complex interactions in mechani-

cal, organic, and social systems so that one can both understand them and manipulate the key factors. A general system has certain basic components that can serve as organizers of a course or unit. There are:

a. Boundaries

b. Component parts

c. Flow (of energy, matter, information, etc.)

d. Interactions

e. Feedback

f. Input/Thruput/Output

Three general systems students come in contact with every day are: family, school, and classroom.

6. Any futures instruction should stress at least two overarching generalizations: (1) time is a process that involves the dimensions of past, present, and future, and (2) future prospects are best viewed from the perspective of multiple, alternative scenarios, rather than the simplistic use of lists of single events or the advocacy of a single scenario or the use of only contrasting positive and negative scenarios.

7. A famous futures think-tank, the Hudson Institute, founded by the late Herman Kahn, has produced a futures course for use at the upper elementary grades through the high school. The course, called "Visions of the Future," contains five units: (1) Time, (2) Earth, (3) Futurology, (4) Problems and Solving, and (5) Where To? The table of contents for the student text follows:[126]

How To Think About The Future
        What *Visions of the Future* Is About
        Views of the Future
        Activities: How to Think About the Future

The Great Transition
        One Vision of the Past, Present, and Future
        Making the Transition
        The Pre-Industrial Stage of the Great Transition
        The Industrial Stage of the Great Transition
        The Post-Industrial Stage of the Great Transition
        Summary
        Activities: The Great Transition

Resources for the Future
        A New Way of Looking at Resources
        Resource Issue 1: Are We Running Out of Raw Materials?
        Resource Issue 2: Will There Be Enough Energy?
        Resource Issue 3: Will There Be Enough Food?
        Resource Issue 4: Will We Make Good Decisions About Our Environment?
        Summary
        Activities: Resources for the Future

Problem Solving in a Time of Change
        Social Limits to Growth
        Problem Solving in a Time of Change
        Understanding Global Problems

Mostly Understandable Problems
Basically Uncertain Problems
Your Contribution
Careers of the Future
Managers of the Future
Activities: Problem Solving in a Time of Change

8. In the *Bulletin* of the World Future Society, Elliott Seif suggest "Seven Dimensions of a Future Living Education." These are:[127]

a. Thinking
b. Feeling
c. Communicating/Expressing
d. Relating
e. Growing
f. Believing
g. Knowing (human condition; societal heritage; global issues; future studies; careers and lifestyles; science, mathematics and technology; survival (e.g., nutrition); esthetics; self)

9. Another configuration for a futures course/unit centers on the broad concept of "Balance." This is an ecological approach in which "Balance" is looked at in regard to six topics: (1) Growth of Populations (in human and natural systems), (2) Matter and Energy (fossil, fission, fusion, and solar sources), (3) Cycles (life, food, historical, and other cyles), (4) Change (gradual, rapid, periodic, etc.), (5) Adaptations (hereditary, biological, etc.), and (6) Interdependence (human, natural, and international webs).

10. For teachers who prefer extensive activity-oriented units, the following list of possible student and class projects may prove useful:

a. A city newspaper in the year 2010
b. An architectural model of a school in the twenty-first century
c. A model home for the next century
d. Help-wanted and classified ads for a newspaper in 2020
e. Proposed bills for action by Congress or a state legislature
f. A Delphi poll of students in a school
g. Interviews with workers in futures occupations
h. Mock-ups of robots

Futures in Elementary and Secondary Schools

In the elementary school curriculum, one unit per grade level (grades 1-6) is probably a feasible optimum. Such units should probably be integrated into the entire curriculum, cutting across such subjects as social studies, science, and language arts. Each unit should provide for the simultaneous pursuit of multiple objectives and could be developed by a "mix and match" usage of the preceding categories/topics lists.

Teachers at this level might find the following topics appropriate sources of futures units and activities:

1. Concepts of time: the continuum from past to present to future—as manifest in a child's lifetime and in the lifetimes of the child's family: mother and father, grandparents and great grandparents, siblings and peers, future friends, husband or wife, and expected offspring (perhaps using life cycles and birth-life-death timelines).

2. Futures we take for granted: the seasons, the motions of our solar system, almanac forecasts of climate, daily routines (breakfast, lunch, dinner, the school schedule, sleep, favorite television shows).

3. Discontinuities or changes that affect us: death in the family; friends who move away; siblings who go away to camp, college, work; wars and depressions; personal accidents (broken arm) and diseases (chicken pox).

4. Fascination with and anticipation of the new: presents at birthdays and holidays, new family acquisitions such as car and television set, a new baby in the family, new toys (perhaps having students design new toys or soft drinks).

5. Coming events: in family, school, and community (perhaps focusing on factors that could cause postponements, cancellations, or delays).

6. Fascinating and curious current events: return of Soviet cosmonauts Lyakhov and Ryumin from record 175 days of living in space (discussing their daily routines and unusual or surprising events), NASA's Pioneer 11 flying "close" by the planet Saturn (photographs of planet and its moons, is there life on the moon Titan?).

7. Home/family energy use and conservation: amounts and types of energy used; conservation measures like insulation, storm windows, weather-stripping.

8. Exponential growth and its effects: stories of doubling times—lily pads in a pond, 64-square chess board.

Probably the greatest asset to introducing futures study into the elementary school is the multidisciplinary nature of the teaching: most elementary teachers teach almost all subjects in the curriculum. This is an advantage because the study of the future is also, by its very nature, multidisciplinary.

Secondary school teachers have many futures curriculum options. Courses or units may be included in the offerings of English, science, and social studies departments. A course can be jointly offered (and team taught) in two or three subject areas: English and social studies, *or* English and science, *or* science and social studies, *or* English, social studies, and science.

5. THREE SELECTED BIBLIOGRAPHIES

The final section of this monograph on future studies is comprised of three selected bibliographies, the first of which is annotated. These are by no means comprehensive lists of citations, but they do provide teachers and other curriculum developers with rather carefully screened and hopefully useful listings.

Because of the breadth and scope of the futures field (even in its infancy), someone's favorite work has undoubtedly been omitted. The author apologizes in advance for such oversights—they are inevitable.

The titles and major subheadings of each of the bibliographies are outlined below:

A Brief Basic Bibliography on the Future (readings for the teacher and curriculum developer)

A Selected Bibliography on Futures Topics

1. General Background on Futures Topics
2. Communication and Transportation
3. Community and Habitat
4. Education
5. Energy and Other Natural Resources
6. Family Life
7. Food and Agriculture
8. Government and Economics
9. Health
10. International Affairs
11. Values, Attitudes, and Lifestyles
12. Work and Leisure

A Future Studies Curriculum Bibliography

1. Methods Books
2. Course and Unit Textbooks
3. Science Fiction

A Brief Basic Bibliography on the Future

Barney, G. D. *The Global 2000 Report to the President.* New York: Penguin, 1980.

This is a U.S. government study commissioned by President Carter and completed under President Reagan. Its scope is the world in the year 2000, and it focuses on such crucial factors as population, natural resources, and pollution. Conclusions indicate a dismal scenario if certain present trends are not curbed.

Bell, D. *The Coming of Post-Industrial Society.* New York: Basic Books, 1973.

Daniel Bell is one of the early theorists in the modern futures movement. He is best known for his popularization of the concept of "postindustrial society." This is probably his best-known work, in which he describes stages in the development of Western civilization: from preindustrial society (i.e., agrarian society) to industrial society to postindustrial society (i.e., information and service society).

Botkin, J. W., et al. *No Limits to Learning.* New York: Pergamon Press (A Club of Rome volume), 1979.

The Club of Rome has commissioned more than a dozen studies on worldwide issues, the most famous of which was *The Limits to Growth*, a doomsday bombshell that appeared just about the time of the oil embargo in 1973-74. *No Limits to Learning* is the first Club study having to do with education. After describing the "human gap" in learning, it advocates "innovative" learning over "maintenance" learning.

Brown, L. R. *The Twenty-Ninth Day.* New York: W.W. Norton, 1978.

This volume by the president of the Worldwatch Institute may be the best overview of the global problematique, the interaction between population and natural resources. Written in a flowing style and using language all can understand, it should appeal to any teacher interested in ecological principles.

Brown, L. R. *Building a Sustainable Society.* New York: W.W. Norton, 1981.

Lester Brown is known for his ecological concerns in the global arena, and most of his writings call attention to major problems and issues. In this work, he describes a positive set of criteria for modifying any extant society so that its culture and lifestyle can be sustained into the distant future. Of particular concern is assuring that strategic natural resources are not prematurely depleted.

Brown, L. R. *State of the World: 1988.* New York: W.W. Norton, 1988.

The publications of the Worldwatch Institute have gained the reputation of being reliable estimates of the current status of worldwide issues. In 1984, the staff of the Institute under the direction of their president, Lester Brown, began producing an annual update on critical global issues. These appear a little before or after January 1st of each year, and the current volume is for 1988. Available in either hardcover or paperback, it makes an excellent textbook for any globally-oriented futures course at the secondary school level.

Capra, F. *The Turning Point.* New York: Simon and Schuster, 1982.

The author of *The Tao of Physics* sees a relationship between our inability to understand quantum mechanics and our faltering ability to deal with current social crises. The problem, as he sees it, is one of perception. We need to embrace a new paradigm, a new vision of reality, new ideas and new values. The pieces of the new paradigm have been emerging for the past 25 years, but have not as yet been unified into a coherent conceptual framework. Capra sees this book as a first step in the development of a new unified theory.

Cetron, M., and T. O'Toole. *Encounters With the Future.* New York: McGraw-Hill, 1982.

These authors present an upbeat view of the next 20 years: "Despite the problems and perils of the human condition, ...most of the world's people will go right on improving their lot." Chapters deal with social shock, life expectancy, energy sources, global economics, prospects for war/peace, religion, telecommunications, robotics, work/jobs, and the space program.

Clarke, A. C. *July 20, 2019: Life in the 21st Century.* New York: Macmillan, 1986.

A venerable futurist and science fiction writer, Clarke looks 50 years beyond the first U.S. moon landing to a time when he envisions there will be lunar inhabitants. In a blend of solid forecasting and plausible speculative fiction, the author describes life in the next century: in homes, in hospitals, in schools, in the lives of robots, in movie theaters, in sports arenas, in offices, in war, in death—and in the bedroom.

Cornish, E., and staff of the World Future Society. *The Study of the Future.* Washington, DC: World Future Society, 1977.

The major author of this basic introductory textbook is known worldwide as the founder and president of the World Future Society. In this volume, the parameters of the futures field are presented, as well as the views of leading futurists and the research methods they use to investigate the future. This paperback bargain is frequently used in high school and college futures courses.

Didsbury, H. F. (ed.). *Communications and the Future.* Washington, DC: World Future Society, 1982.

This volume is one of eight or so derived from "annual" (not always every year) conferences of the World Future Society. It comprises selected speeches and papers presented at the 1981 conference, which had as its theme, "communications." Although the conference books are uneven in quality of selections, this one is particularly good due to the theme and many excellent articles organized under three headings: Prospects, Promises, and Problems.

Didsbury, H. F. (ed.). *Creating a Global Agenda.* Washington, DC: World Future Society, 1984.

Another WFS conference collection, this work is particularly useful because of its international emphasis. Included are sections on Reducing the Nuclear Peril, Elements of a Peaceful World, Responses to Technological Change, Early Warning Signals, and A Common Global Project. The authors of the selected papers are among the elite of the modern futures movement.

Didsbury, H. F. (ed.). *Challenges and Opportunities: From Now to 2110.* Washington, DC: World Future Society, 1986.

The articles in this volume are from the 1986 New York City conference of WFS. They are organized around six topics: Crisis Management and Conflict Resolution, Progress Toward Mutual Global Security, Roots of Potential Conflict, Economics: Differing Perspectives, Continuous Education for a Changing World, and Wider Boundaries for More Effective Management. Although this collection hangs together weakly, it is the latest in the WFS series.

Elgin, D. *Voluntary Simplicity.* New York: William Morrow, 1981.

In the tradition of a Buddhist economy and lifestyle, Elgin advocates a lowered standard of living for those living in the "over-developed" nations such as the United States, West Germany, and Japan. For most of its existence on the planet, the human species has lived a modest lifestyle, relying on the land and ingenuity for survival. The author argues that a high quality of life and community can occur only if the developed world voluntarily chooses to live a simpler existence.

Ellul, J. *The Technological Society.* New York: Alfred Knopf, 1964.

This work is now a classic in the sociological and philosophical treatment of the role of technology in society. Ellul explores several definitions of the ubiquitous concept, "technique." He sees all modern societies as slaves to the machine, but, more devastatingly, he views technology as more than mere machines. Technique is *the* way of doing things, of solving problems, and as such pervades all modes of existence. The tragedy is that alternative ways of coping with and solving problems are discredited in the face of the appeal of technique.

Evans, C. *The Micro Millenium.* New York: Viking Press, 1979.

Evans presents a superb overview of "The Computer Revolution," especially since the advent of the personal microcomputer in the mid-70s. He begins with a brief history of computing machines, describes the "present" (i.e., 1979), and forecasts quite accurately the personal computer evolution during the 1980s. Finally, he describes the emergence of expert systems and artificial intelligence and even speculates on the nature of the computer in the next century.

Ferguson, M. *The Aquarian Conspiracy: Personal and Social Transformation in the 1980s.* New York: J.P. Tarcher/St. Martin's Press, 1980.

Ferguson is a master of the art of synthesis, and in this popular work she weaves together the strands of many seemingly disparate mini-movements into what she argues is a significant paradigm shift in U.S. society. The "conspiracy" is the underground nature of an incredible variety of non-establishment groups, all working to subvert current societal trends and values — all in the Age of Aquarius.

Fitch, R. M., and C. M. Svengalis. *Futures Unlimited.* Washington, DC: National Council for the Social Studies (Bulletin 59), 1979.

One of four or five future studies methods books, this is one of the best and most useful. For the teacher planning a unit or course on the future at the elementary or secondary level, this short booklet is an indispensable tool. Excellent bibliographies (for a 1979 edition), one of which is annotated, are included.

Fuller, R. B. *Operating Manual for Spaceship Earth.* New York: Pocket Books, 1969.

This delightful short "history" of Western civilization is by one of the unique minds of this century, a model futurist who throughout his long life constantly demonstrated creative and comprehensive thinking. In this work "Bucky" makes the telling point that, unlike modern automobiles, planet Earth came without an operating manual. As a result, we the users have been slow to learn how the system operates, but if we don't discover the crucial principles soon, it may become uninhabitable.

Fuller, R. B. *Critical Path.* New York: St. Martin's Press, 1981.

Written while Fuller was in his 80s, this thick volume describes his analysis of the world's major problems and his illumination of the "critical path" we must take to avoid destruction on our planet. The going is sometimes difficult due to Fuller's cryptic prose, but this is relieved somewhat by his poignant parables.

Harman, W. W. *An Incomplete Guide to the Future.* New York: W.W. Norton, 1976.

As a prototype transformationist, Harman in this work first presents a critique of the current "industrial paradigm," then outlines four major modern dilemmas (growth, work-roles, world distribution, and control), gives a brilliant speculation on the human potential, and ends with a description of "transindustrial society" and how we can arrive there.

Harman, W. W., and H. Rheingold. *Higher Creativity.* Boston: Houghton Mifflin, 1984.

In this book, Harman's most recent, he (with his co-author) further amplifies his ideas on human evolution—especially in the realms of creativity and spirituality. Again as a transformationist, he points to "a new Copernican Revolution," a new system break or paradigm shift, which will unshackle the immense capabilities of the human being.

Hawken, P., J. Ogilvy, and P. Schwartz. *Seven Tomorrows.* New York: Bantam Books, 1982.

Sprightly, mostly serious, though occasionally humorous, this product of SRI International (a leading U.S. "futures shop") looks at six possible alternative scenarios to "The Official Future" (a straight extrapolation of current U.S. trends). The six are: Mature Calm, Apocalyptic Transformation, and Living Within Our Means (three scenarios based on frugal values); and The Center Holds, Chronic Breakdown, and Beginnings of Sorrow (all based on survival values).

Kahn, H. *World Economic Development.* New York: William Morrow, 1979.

An upbeat extrapolationist and anti-doomsday futurist, the late Herman Kahn founded the famous Hudson Institute and presented over the past 30 years a series of growth/development/progress scenarios for America and the world. As economic growth is sustained in the developed world, Kahn sees progress for the developing world through a trickle-down effect. He is an avid believer in capitalism and sees Japan, South Korea, and Taiwan as new, successful, Asian converts and exemplars of this economic ideology.

Kahn, H. *The Coming Boom.* New York: Simon and Schuster, 1982.

This was Kahn's last work prior to his death a few years ago, and the title is consistent with his economic outlook over the past three or four decades. It is a U.S. scenario, but with ramifications for the rest of the developed and the developing worlds. He looks at "high tech," inflation, national debts, energy, defense policy, and politics, but his theme is the need for "revitalization" of the American economy.

Leonard, G. B. *The Transformation: A Guide to the Inevitable Changes in Humankind.* New York: Delacorte, 1972.

As his title suggests, Leonard is a transformationist, who, like Willis Harman, holds that the major feature of the future will be new realizations of human potentiality. Leonard's thesis is that the present age is unique and will bring a "thorough going change in the quality of human existence." But there is both joy and pain to personal and societal changes, and the new age will have a difficult birth.

Mitchell, A. *The Nine American Lifestyles.* New York: Warner, 1983.

Another product of the SRI International research and demonstration shop, this provocative study grows out of survey research (800 questions, 1,600 subjects). Mitchell claims that today in the United States there are nine discrete lifestyles that cluster in four groupings:

    I.   The Need-Driven Groups—1. Survivors; 2. Sustainers
    II.   The Outer-Directed Groups—3. Belongers; 4. Emulators; 5. Achievers
    III.   The Inner-Directed Groups—6. I-AM-ME; 7. Experiential; 8. Societally Conscious
    IV.   The Combined Outer- and Inner-Directed Group—9. Integrated

Mumford, L. *The Transformations of Man.* New York: Harper, 1956.

Lewis Mumford is one of those rare "Renaissance" persons whose mind ranges over many idea landscapes. One is tempted to say anything he writes is worth reading! Here he traces the historical evolution of humans and their societies through eight transformations, from "Animal Into Human" to

"World Culture." It's a well-written tour de force covering a million years of evolution and six thousand years of human societies.

Naisbitt, J. *Megatrends.* New York: Warner, 1982.

A futures bestseller in the 1980s, Naisbitt's book identifies ten "megatrends" in the U.S. today. Each is presented as a shift "from" one condition "to" another. The trends are (1) From an Industrial Society to an Information Society, (2) Forced Technology to High Tech/High Touch (i.e., computers plus human relations), (3) National to World Economy, (4) Short Term Planning to Long Term, (5) Centralization (i.e., urban and bureaucratic) to Decentralization, (6) Institutional Help (e.g., schools and hospitals) to Self-Help, (7) Representative Democracy to Participatory Democracy, (8) Hierarchies to Networks, (9) North (East and Midwest) to South (Southeast and Southwest), and (10) Either/or Choices to Multiple Options.

O'Neill, G. K. *2081.* New York: Simon and Schuster, 1981.

A Princeton physicist, O'Neill is best known as the popularizer of the potential of space colonies. In this forecast of the next 100 years, he argues that there are five major "drivers of change" for U.S. society: (1) space colonies, (2) computers, (3) energy, (4) automation, and (5) communications. As might be guessed, O'Neill is an extrapolationist with enormous confidence in technology as the single most potent force for change.

Ophuls, W. *Ecology and the Politics of Scarcity.* San Francisco: W. H. Freeman, 1977.

This work is an excellent, concise treatment of the issue of scarcity (of everything, but especially of natural resources). If most things are scarce, societies and individuals need to accept the constraint imposed by limits to growth and progress. The result of accepting limits is the emergence of "a steady-state economy" within a stable society.

Oxford Analytica. *America In Perspective.* Boston: Houghton Mifflin, 1986.

Written by a team of Oxford, U.K. scholars/consultants, this extensive treatment of the future of American society paints a realistic portrait of the strengths and weaknesses of U.S. society and projects trends to the next century. Part I portrays society: demographic trends, standards of living, mobility of social classes, attitudes toward work, the family and the role of women, "the rural ethic," and changes in religion and values. Part II explores politics: new power centers, pressure groups, the media, political parties, three branches of federal governance, and changing political attitudes and ideologies. Part III deals with the economy: productivity, unemployment, monetary and fiscal policies, and the federal budget deficit. Part IV looks into the 1990s via eight "Themes of the Future."

Roszak, T. *Person/Planet.* New York: Anchor/Doubleday, 1978.

Roszak is a radical classics scholar and intellectual historian, who laments the directions taken by modern society and who looks to "the creative disintegration of industrial society" as a necessary traumatic and anarchic transition to a new age. In this work, he argues that transformationists should focus on the levels of personhood and planetscope, while accepting the necessity of the destruction of current obsolete societies, i.e., nation-states.

Salk, J. *The Survival of the Wisest.* New York: Harper and Row, 1973.

Nobel laureate (for polio vaccine) Salk shifts his focus from medical science to the threats to survival of the human species. Giving a twist to a famous phrase of Charles Darwin, he suggests it will be the "wisest" rather than the "fittest" who will survive in the next century. Using the metaphor of an S-shaped curve (or sigmoid curve as he calls it), he suggests that exponential growth, the first half of the S-curve, marks human history up to today. We are now at the point of inflection, after which exponential growth will continue to disasters and the end of life or we will reverse the first half of the curve and move toward slowed growth and eventual stability in a steady-state world.

Theobald, R. *The Rapids of Change.* Indianapolis: Knowledge Systems, 1987.

Another Renaissance person, Theobald dislikes labels describing his "specializations": economist, internationalist, futurist, and prolific writer. In this, his most recent work, he suggests ways citizens can engage in "social entrepreneurship in turbulent times." He might be best described as a realistic transformationist who fervently believes individuals need to act on their world to feel efficacy in life. This book is a guide to modes of individual and collective action persons can take to bring to fruition futures they prefer.

Thompson, W. I. *Darkness and Scattered Light.* New York: Anchor/Doubleday, 1978.

A dropout M.I.T. history professor, Thompson has been writing about the "impending" transformation of Western culture since his 1971 work, *At the Edge of History.* In this gloomy forecast, he argues that there is much "darkness" (i.e., misery and discontent) in modern developed societies, with only the occasional ray of "scattered light" in personal lifestyles and communal modes of living. The promise lies in a significant minority of persons and groups who practice "small but beautiful," voluntary simplicity, and "appropriate" technology.

Toffler, A. *Future Shock.* New York: Random House, 1970.

Almost singlehandedly, Toffler is responsible for the resurgence of futures study in the present age, mainly through the publication of this book, in English and in dozens of other languages. Although it is a classic in the field, the writing is shallow and the analysis simplistic, yet it tapped a feeling in the modern reader with its emphasis on the shock and disorientation of rapid change.

Toffler, A. *The Third Wave.* New York: William Morrow, 1980.

In this work, Toffler the transitionist describes three waves of change, three revolutions that overwhelmed humanity: First Wave—The Agricultural Revolution; Second Wave—The Industrial Revolution; and Third Wave—The Communications Revolution. In the Third Wave, Toffler foresees more presentism, less "massification," less work time/more leisure time, smaller families, improved human relations, greater adaptability, flextime, the electronic cottage, extensive telecommunications, more concern for both self-fulfillment/self-esteem/self-reliance and feelings of community.

World Future Society

The WFS is a rich mine of resources for both the novice and experienced futurist. Its journal is *The Futurist*, a non-technical, popular showcase for timely articles on a multitude of topics. In its Bookstore column (and "The Futurist Bookstore," a seasonal brochure listing over a hundred books, games, and tapes), it advertises recent books at reduced prices to members. It also publishes special collections of articles from *The Futurist* in single bound books; edited volumes of selected papers from annual WFS conferences; *Future Survey* and *Future Survey Annual*, abstracts by selected topics of articles and books on the future; and *Futures Research Quarterly*, a more technical research-oriented journal. Periodically WFS updates its reference work on individuals, institutions, and publications with futures interests, *The Future: A Guide to Information Sources.*

Yankelovich, D. *New Rules.* New York: Random House, 1981.

This report of survey research describes changing values in American society at the beginning of the 1980s. The chief value Yankelovich focuses on is "the self-fulfillment ethic." This value is a reversal of the long-dominant cluster of American values subsumed in The Protestant Ethic. Since self-fulfillment is a form of individualism, the author worries about the discrediting of the value of communalism or common concern, and hopes there will emerge a new balance in what he calls the "Giving/Getting Compact."

A Selected Bibliography on Futures Topics

1. General Background on Futures Topics

Beckwith, B. P. *The Next 500 Years.* New York: Exposition Press, 1967.

Boulding, K. E. *The Meaning of the Twentieth Century.* New York: Harper Colophon, 1964.

Boyer, W. *America's Future: Transition to the 21st Century.* New York: Praeger, 1984.

Cornish, E. (ed.). *Global Solutions.* Washington, DC: World Future Society, 1984.

Gallup, G. *Forecast 2000.* New York: William Morrow, 1986.

Hartmann, W., R. Miller, and P. Lee. *Out of the Cradle: Exploring the Frontiers Beyond Earth.* New York: Workman, 1984.

Hughes, B. *World Futures.* Baltimore: Johns Hopkins University Press, 1985.

Kurtzman, J. *Futurcasting.* Palm Springs, CA: ETC Publications, 1984.

Long, K. *The American Forecaster: 1987.* Philadelphia: Running Press, 1986.

Marien, M. *Societal Directions and Alternatives: A Critical Guide to the Literature.* LaFayette, NY: Information for Policy Design, 1976.

Stableford, B., and D. Langford. *The Third Millennium.* New York: Alfred Knopf, 1985.

World Future Society Staff. *Futures Research Directory: Individuals.* Washington, DC: World Future Society, 1987.

2. Communication and Transportation

Bagdikian, B. H. *The Information Machines: Their Impact on Man and the Media.* New York: Harper and Row, 1971.

Cornish, E. (ed.). *Communications Tomorrow.* Washington, DC: World Future Society, 1982.

Cornish, E. (ed.). *The Computerized Society.* Washington, DC: World Future Society, 1985.

Glossbrenner, A. *The Complete Handbook of Personal Computer Communications.* New York: St. Martin's Press, 1985.

Didsbury, H. (ed.). *Communications and the Future.* Washington, DC: World Future Society, 1982.

Forester, T. *The Information Technology Revolution.* Cambridge, MA: MIT Press, 1985.

Masuda, Y. *The Information Society as Post-Industrial Society.* Washington, DC: World Future Society, 1981.

Miller, A. R. *The Assault on Privacy: Computers, Data Banks, and Dossiers.* Ann Arbor, MI: University of Michigan Press, 1971.

National Commission on Space. *Pioneering the Space Frontier.* New York: Bantam, 1986.

Pureitt, M. *Art and the Computer.* New York: McGraw-Hill, 1984.

3. Community and Habitat

Campbell, C.C. *New Towns: Another Way to Live.* Reston, VA: 1976.

Cornish E. (ed.). *Habitats Tomorrow.* Washington, DC: World Future Society, 1984.

Cowley, S. *Spacebase 2000.* New York: St. Martin's Press, 1985.

Critchfield, R. *Villages.* New York: Anchor/Doubleday, 1981.

Doxiadas, C. *Ekistics: An Introduction to the Science of Human Settlements.* New York: Oxford, 1968.

Maruyama, M., and A. Harkins (eds.). *Cultures Beyond the Earth.* New York: Vintage, 1975.

Melville, K. *Communes in the Counterculture: Origins, Theories, Styles of Life.* New York: William Morrow, 1972.

O'Neill, G. K. *The High Frontier: Human Colonies in Space.* New York: William Morrow, 1977.

Robinson, G., and H. White. *Envoys of Mankind.* Washington, DC: Smithsonian Institution Press, 1986.

Stine, G. H. *Handbook for Space Colonists.* New York: Holt, Rinehart and Winston, 1985.

4. Education

Botkin, J., M. Elmandjra, and M. Malitz. *No Limits to Learning.* New York: Pergamon Press, 1979.

Bowman, J., et al. *The Far Side of the Future.* Washington, DC: World Future Society, 1978.

Hudspeth, D., and R. Brey. *Instructional Telecommunications.* New York: Praeger, 1986.

Cetron, M. *Schools of the Future.* New York: McGraw-Hill, 1985.

Jennings, L., and S. Cornish (eds.). *Education and the Future.* Washington, DC: World Future Society, 1980.

Hawkridge, D. *New Information Technology in Education.* Baltimore: Johns Hopkins University Press, 1983.

Kierstead, F., J. Bowman, and C. Dede. *Educational Futures: Sourcebook I.* Washington, DC: World Future Society, 1979.

Michael D. *On Learning to Plan and Planning to Learn.* San Francisco: Jossey-Bass, 1973.

Redd, K., and A. Harkins. *Education: A Time for Decisions.* Washington, DC: World Future Society, 1980.

Rubin, L. (ed.). *The Future of Education.* New York: Allyn and Bacon, 1975.

Samples, B. *The Metaphoric Mind.* Reading, MA: Addison-Wesley, 1976.

Shane, H. G. *Curriculum Change Toward the 21st Century.* Washington, DC: National Education Association, 1977.

Shane, H. G. *Educating for a New Millenium.* Bloomington, IN: Phi Delta Kappa, 1981.

Shane H. G. *Teaching and Learning in a Microelectronic Age.* Bloomington, IN: Phi Delta Kappa, 1987.

Sullivan, E. A. *The Future: Human Ecology and Education.* Palm Springs, CA: ETC Publications, 1975.

5. Energy and Other Natural Resources

Commoner, B. *The Closing Circle.* New York: Alfred Knopf, 1971.

Dahlberg, K. *Environment and the Global Arena.* Durham, NC: Duke University Press, 1985.

Ehrlich, P. R., and A. H. Ehrlich. *Population, Resources, Environment: Issues in Human Ecology.* San Francisco: W. H. Freeman, 1970.

Gabel, M. *Energy, Earth and Everyone.* San Francisco: Straight Arrow Books, 1975.

Jungk, R. *The Everyman Project: A World Report on the Resources for a Humane Society.* New York: Liveright, 1977.

Nuclear Energy Policy Study Group. *Nuclear Power: Issues and Choices.* Cambridge, MA: Ballinger, 1977.

Platt, J. *Perception and Change: Projections for Survival.* Ann Arbor, MI: The University of Michigan Press, 1970.

Repetto, R. *The Global Possible: Resources, Development, and the New Century.* New Haven, CT: Yale University Press, 1985.

Schneider, S. H. *The Genesis Strategy: Climate and Global Survival.* New York: Plenum Press, 1976.

Workshop on Alternative Energy Strategies. *Energy: Global Prospects, 1985-2000.* New York: McGraw-Hill, 1977.

6. Family Life

Bernard, J. *The Future of Marriage.* New York: Bantam, 1972.

Francoeur, R. T., and A. K. Francoeur. *The Future of Sexual Relations.* Englewood Cliffs, NJ: Prentice-Hall, 1974.

Newland, K., and P. McGrath. *The Sisterhood of Man: Women's Changing Roles in a Changing World.* New York: W. W. Norton, 1980.

Otto, H. *The Family in Search of a Future.* New York: Dell, 1974.

7. Food and Agriculture

Brown, L. R., and E. Eckholm. *By Bread Alone.* New York: Praeger, 1974.

Ford, B. *Future Food: Alternative Protein for the Year 2000.* New York: William Morrow, 1978.

Lappe, F. M. *Diet for a Small Planet.* New York: Ballantine, 1975.

Shepherd, J. *The Politics of Starvation.* Washington, DC: Carnegie Endowment for International Peace, 1975.

8. Government and Economics

Baier, K., and N. Rescher (eds.). *Values and the Future.* New York: Free Press, 1970.

Burhoe, R. (ed.). *Science and Human Values in the 21st Century.* Philadelphia: Westminster Press, 1971.

Derr, C. B. *Managing the New Careerists.* San Francisco: Jossey-Bass, 1986.

Ferkiss, V. *The Future of Technological Civilization.* New York: George Braziller, 1974.

Hawken, P. *The Next Economy.* New York: Ballentine, 1983.

Schumacher, E. F. *Small Is Beautiful.* New York: Harper and Row, 1973.

Toffler, A. *The Adaptive Corporation.* New York: McGraw-Hill, 1985.

9. Health

Bezold, C. (ed.). *Pharmacy in the 21st Century.* Washington, DC: Institute for Alternative Futures, 1985.

Colen, B. *Hard Choices: Mixed Blessings of Modern Medical Technology.* New York: Putnam, 1986.

Drexler, K. *Engines of Creation.* New York: Anchor/Doubleday, 1986.

Maxmen, J. S. *The Post-Physician Era: Medicine in the Twenty-First Century.* New York: John Wiley, 1976.

Olson, S. *Biotechnology: An Industry Comes of Age.* Washington, DC: National Academy Press, 1986.

Pifer, A., and L. Bronte. *Our Aging Society.* New York: W. W. Norton, 1986.

Rosenfeld, A. *The Second Genesis: The Coming Control of Life.* Englewood Cliffs, NJ: Prentice-Hall, 1969.

Rosenfeld, A. *Prolongevity.* New York: Alfred Knopf, 1976.

Rosenfeld, A. *Prolengevity II.* New York: Alfred Knopf, 1985.

Salomon, M. *Future Life.* New York: Macmillan, 1983.

Teresi, D., and P. Adcroft (eds.). *Omni's Future Medical Almanac.* New York: McGraw-Hill, 1987.

10. International Affairs

Barnet, R., and R.E. Mullen. *Global Reach: The Power of the Multinational Corporations.* New York: Simon and Schuster, 1974.

Boulding, K. *The World As a Total System.* New York: Sage, 1985.

Brown, L. R. *World Without Borders.* New York: Random House, 1972.

Brown, L.R., P. McGrath, and B. Stokes. *Twenty-Two Dimensions of the Population Problem.* Washington, DC: Worldwatch Institute (Paper 5), 1976.

Copeland, L., and L. Griggs, *Going International.* New York: Random House, 1985.

Laszlo, E., et al. *Goals for Mankind.* New York: New American Library, 1977.

Lovins, A. *Soft Energy Paths.* Cambridge, MA: Ballinger, 1977.

McHale, J., and M. McHale. *Basic Human Needs: A Framework for Action.* Houston, TX: Center for Integrative Studies, 1977.

Mendlovitz, S. *On the Creation of a Just World Order.* New York: Free Press, 1975

Mesarovic, M., and E. Pestel. *Mankind at the Turning Point.* New York: E.P. Dutton and Reader's Digest Press, 1974.

Tinbergen, J., et al. *RIO: Reshaping the International Order.* New York: E. P. Dutton, 1976.

11. Values, Attitudes, and Lifestyles

Baier, K., and N. Rescher (eds.). *Values and the Future.* New York: Free Press, 1970.

Burhoe, R. (ed.). *Science and Human Values in the 21st Century.* Philadelphia. Westminster Press, 1971.

Derr, C. B. *Managing the New Careerists.* San Francisco: Jossey-Bass, 1986.

Inglehart, R. *The Silent Revolution.* Princeton: Princeton University Press, 1977.

Mead, M. *Culture and Commitment.* New York: Doubleday, 1970.

Pelletier, K. *Toward a Science of Consciousness.* New York: Dell, 1978.

Roszak, T. *Unfinished Animal.* New York: Harper and Row, 1976.

Rougemont, D. *The Future Is Within Us.* New York: Pergamon, 1983.

Russell, P. *The Global Brain.* Los Angeles: J. P. Tarcher, 1983.

Schumacher, E.F. *A Guide for the Perplexed.* New York: Harper and Row, 1977.

Targ, R., and H. Puthoff. *Mind-Reach.* New York: Dell, 1977.

Yankelovich, D. *New Rules.* New York: Random House, 1981.

12. Work and Leisure

Ashford, N. *Crisis in the Workplace.* Cambridge, MA: MIT Press, 1976.

Ayres, R., and S. Miller. *Robotics: Applications and Social Implications.* New York: Ballinger, 1983.

Best, F. (ed.). *The Future of Work.* Englewood Cliffs, NJ: Prentice-Hall, 1973.

Cetron, M. *Jobs of the Future.* New York: McGraw-Hill, 1984.

Cornish E. (ed.). *Careers Tomorrow.* Washington, DC: World Future Society, 1983.

Dickson, P. *The Future of the Workplace.* New York: Weybright and Talley, 1976.

Didsbury, H. (ed.). *The World of Work: Careers and the Future.* Washington, DC: World Future Society, 1983.

Hirschhorn, L. *Beyond Mechanization: Work and Technology in a Postindustrial Age.* Cambridge, MA: MIT Press, 1984.

Johansen, R. *Teleconferencing and Beyond.* New York: McGraw-Hill, 1984.

Maus, R., and R. Allsup. *Robotics: A Manager's Guide.* New York: Wiley, 1986.

O'Toole, J. (ed.). *Work in America.* Cambridge, MA: MIT Press, 1973.

Sheppard, H., and R. Herrick. *Where Have All the Robots Gone?* New York: Free Press, 1972.

Sigel, E. *The Future of Videotext.* Englewood Cliffs, NJ: Prentice-Hall, 1983.

A Future Studies Curriculum Bibliography

1. Methods Books

Fitch, R., and C. Svengalis. *Futures Unlimited.* Washington, DC: National Council for the Social Studies (Bulletin 59), 1979.

Heinz, B., et al. *Tomorrow, and Tomorrow, and Tomorrow...* New York: Holt, Rinehart and Winston, 1974.

Kauffman, D. *Futurism and Future Studies.* Washington, DC: National Education Association, 1976.

Kauffman, D. *Teaching the Future.* Palm Springs, CA: ETC Publications, 1976.

Laconte, R., and E. Laconte. *Teaching Tomorrow Today.* New York: Bantam, 1975.

Toffler, A. (ed.). *Learning for Tomorrow.* New York: Vintage, 1974.

2. Course and Unit Textbooks

Allen, F., et al. *Deciding How to Live on Spaceship Earth.* Winona, MN: St. Mary's College Press, 1973.

Bellamy, E. *Looking Backward: 2000-1887.* New York: Ticknor, 1887 (many recent paperback editions).

Carpenter, J. *Destination Tomorrow.* Dubuque, IA: W. C. Brown, 1972.

Cera, M., et al. *Creating Your Future: Activities to Encourage Thinking Ahead.* Three separate versions: Grades 1-3, Grades 4-6, and Grades 7-9. Tucson, AZ: Kino Publications, 1982.

Didsbury, H. *The Study of the Future: Instructor's Manual.* Washington, DC: World Future Society, 1979.

Didsbury, H. *The Study of the Future: Student Handbook.* Washington, DC: World Future Society, 1979.

Draze, D. *The Future Traveler.* Dandy Lion Publications, 1983. Available from the World Future Society.

Garlan, P. et al. *Star Sight: Visions of the Future.* Englewood Cliffs, NJ: Prentice-Hall, 1977.

Goodykoontz, W. *The Future: Can We Shape It?* New York: Scholastic, 1973.

Haas, J. D., et al. *Teaching About the Future.* Boulder, CO: Social Science Education Consortium and Denver, CO: Center for Teaching International Relations, 1987.

Hellfach, J. *Future Studies: A Systems Approach* (A series of four paperback textbooks with a teaching guide). Englewood Cliffs, NJ: Prentice-Hall, 1977.

> *The Future of the Environment*
> *The Future of the Family*
> *The Future of the Government*
> *The Future of Work*

Leinwand, C. *The Future.* New York: Pocket Books, 1976.

Melnick, R. *Visions of the Future.* Croton-On-Hudson, NY: Hudson Institute, 1984.

Richardson, J. (ed.). *Making It Happen.* U.S. Association for the Club of Rome, 1982. Available from the World Future Society.

Rosen, S. *Future Facts.* New York: Simon and Schuster, 1976.

Roszak, T. *Unfinished Animal.* New York: Harper and Row, 1976.

Schumacher, E. F. *Guide for the Perplexed.* New York: Harper and Row, 1977.

Tanner, J. *Futuristics: Self-Directed Study Units for Grades K-3 and 4-8 (Gifted).* Zephyr Press, 1982. Available from the World Future Society.

Taylor, P. *The Kids' Whole Future Catalog.* New York: Random House, 1982.

Thomas, J. *Making Changes: A Futures-Oriented Course in Inventive Problem-Solving.* Palm Springs, CA: ETC Publications, 1981.

Whaley, C. *Future Studies: Personal and Global Possibilities.* Trillium Press, 1984. Available from the World Future Society.

World Future Society. Many of the WFS publications are suitable as textbooks for junior/senior high school students, e.g., Cornish, E., *Careers Tomorrow.*, 1983.

Yankelovich, D. *New Rules.* New York: Random House, 1981.

3. Science Fiction

Allen, D. *Science Fiction: The Future.* New York: Harcourt, Brace, Jovanovich, 1971.

Asimov, I. *I, Robot.* New York: Pyramid Books, 1970.

Asimov, I. *The Martian Way.* Greenwich, CT: Fawcett, 1969. Almost all of the fiction of Isaac Asimov is well-written, provocative, and based in science.

Clarke, A. *Childhood's End.* New York: Ballantine, 1953.

Clarke, A. *Imperial Earth.* New York: Harcourt, Brace, Jovanovich, 1976. Almost all of the fiction of Arthur C. Clarke is well-written, provocative, and based in science, including the recent series, *2001, 2010,* and *2060.*

Heinlein, R. *Between Planets.* New York: Act Books, 1951.

Heinlein, R. *Citizens of the Galaxy.* New York: Act Books, 1957.

Heinlein, R. *Double Star.* New York: New American Library, 1957.

Heinlein, R. *Methuselah's Children.* New York: New American Library, 1958.

Heinlein, R. *The Moon Is a Harsh Mistress.* New York: Berkeley, 1966.

Herbert F. *Dune.* New York: Ace Books, 1965. Since this original volume, the Dune series now has six books in the chronological sequence.

Huxley, A. *Brave New World.* New York: Harper and Row, 1932.

Huxley, A. *Island.* New York: Bantam Books, 1962.

Merrill, J. *Daughters of Earth.* New York: Dell, 1968.

Miller, W. *A Canticle for Leibowitz.* New York: Lippincott, 1960.

Orwell, G. *1984.* New York: Harcourt, Brace, and World, 1949.

Vonnegut, K., Jr. *Welcome to the Monkey House.* New York: Dell, 1968.

6. REFERENCES

[1]Bartrand de Jouvenal. *The Art of Conjecture*. New York: Basic Books, Inc., 1967, p. 10.

[2]V. C. Ferkiss. *Futurology: Promise, Performance, Prospects*. The Washington Papers, 50, Beverly Hills, CA: Sage Publications, 1977, p. 10.

[3]Edward Cornish, et al. *The Study of the Future*. Washington, DC: World Future Society, 1977, p. 98.

[4]R. Buckminster Fuller. *Operating Manual for Spaceship Earth*. New York: Pocket Books, 1969, p. 42.

[5]*Ibid.*, p. 44.

[6]David C. King. *Interdependence*. New York: Center for War Peace Studies, 1975, p. iv.

[7]"The Future: A Special Supplement," *U.S. News and World Report*, Vol. 94, No. 18 (May 9, 1983), p. A1.

[8]Herman Kahn. *World Economic Development*. New York: Morrow Quill Paperbacks, 1979, pp. 27-30.

[9]*Ibid.*, pp. 27-29.

[10]Gerard K. O'Neill. *The High Frontier: Human Colonies in Space*. New York: Morrow, 1977.

[11]Gerard K. O'Neill. *2081: A Hopeful View of the Human Future.* New York: Simon and Schuster, 1981, p. 20.

[12]*Ibid.*, p. 15.

[13]*Ibid.*, pp. 39-102.

[14]*Ibid.*, p. 42.

[15]*Ibid.*, pp. 50-61

[16]Kahn, *op. cit.*

[17]O'Neill, *2081...*, p. 62.

[18]*Ibid.*, p. 63.

[19]*Ibid.*, pp. 75-94.

[20]*Ibid.*, pp. 94-102.

[21]Jonas Salk. *The Survival of the Wisest*. New York: Harper and Row, 1973.

[22]Daniel Bell. *The Cultural Contradictions of Capitalism*. New York: Harper and Row, Basic Books, 1976, p. 198.

[23]Daniel Bell. *The Coming of Post-Industrial Society*. New York: Basic Books, 1973, pp. 115-119.

[24]*Ibid.*, pp. 115-116.

[25]*Ibid.*, pp. 14, 115-119.

[26] John Naisbitt. *Megatrends*. New York: Warner Books, 1982.

[27] *Ibid.*, p. I.

[28] *Ibid.*, p. 1.

[29] *Ibid.*

[30] *Ibid.*, p. 39.

[31] *Ibid.*, p. 42.

[32] *Ibid.*, p. 1.

[33] *Ibid.*, pp. 79-96.

[34] *Ibid.*, pp. 97-129.

[35] *Ibid.*, pp. 131-157.

[36] *Ibid.*, pp. 159-188.

[37] *Ibid.*, p. 191.

[38] *Ibid.*, p. 192.

[39] *Ibid.*, p. 2.

[40] *Ibid.*, p. 207.

[41] *Ibid.*, pp. 207-229.

[42] *Ibid.*, p. 2.

[43] *Ibid.*, p. 232.

[44] Theodore Roszak. *Unfinished Animal*. New York: Harper Colophon Books, 1975.

[45] *Ibid.*, p. 3.

[46] *Ibid.*, p. 4.

[47] *Ibid.*, pp. 25-29.

[48] *Ibid.*, p. 31.

[49] *Ibid.*, p. 37.

[50] Theodore Roszak. *Person/Planet*. Garden City, NY: Anchor Press/Doubleday, 1978, p. xix.

[51] *Ibid.*, p. 32.

[52] *Ibid.*, pp. 129-282.

[53] Willis W. Harman. *An Incomplete Guide to the Future*. San Francisco: San Francisco Book Co., 1976.

[54]*Ibid.*, p. 25.

[55]*Ibid.*, p. 39.

[56]*Ibid.*, p. 51.

[57]*Ibid.*, p. 67.

[58]*Ibid.*, pp. 79-80.

[59]Gunnarl Myrdal. *An American Dilemma*. New York: Harper and Brothers, 1944, pp. x/viii.

[60]Daniel Bell. *The Cultural Contradictions...*, p. 55.

[61]Van Wyck Brooks. *America's Coming of Age*. Garden City, NY: Doubleday Anchor, 1958, 5.

[62]Daniel Bell. *The Cultural Contradictions...*, p. 57.

[63]*Ibid.*, p. 58.

[64]Max Weber. *The Protestant Ethic and the Spirit of Capitalism*. London: G. Allen & Unwin, 1930.

[65]Daniel Bell. *The Cultural Contradictions...*, pp. 60-61.

[66]Daniel Yankelovich. *New Rules*. NY: Random House, 1981, pp. xviii and 5.

[67]*Ibid.*, p. 89.

[68]*Ibid.*, pp. 93-96.

[69]*Ibid.*, pp. 58-59.

[70]*Ibid.*, p. 184.

[71]*Ibid.*, p. 185.

[72]*Ibid.*, p. 231.

[73]*Ibid.*, p. 246.

[74]*Ibid.*, p. 250.

[75]Arnold Mitchell. *The Nine American Lifestyles*. New York: Macmillan Publishing Co., 1983.

[76]*Ibid.*, p. 3.

[77]*Ibid.*, pp. 4 and 63.

[78]*Ibid.*, p. 201.

[79]*Ibid.*, p. 221.

[80]Edward Cornish, et. al. *The Study of the Future*. Washington, DC: World Future Society, 1977, p. 2.

[81]*Ibid.*, pp. 25-32.

[82]A. B. Migdal. "The Frontiers of Science." In *Einstein* (Special Issue of the UNESCO Courier, Paris, France), s, 1979, p. 29.

[83]Richard D. Van Scotter, Richard J. Kraft, and John D. Haas. *Foundations of Education: Social Perspectives*. Englewood Cliffs, NJ: Prentice-Hall, 1979.

[84]O.W. Markley, et. al. *Changing Images of Man*. Menlo Park, CA: Stanford Research Institute, Center for the Study of Social Policy, Report No. 4, May 1974, p. 92.

[85]*Ibid.*, p. 106.

[86]*Ibid.*, p. 107.

[87]Jacob Bronowski. *The Ascent of Man*. Boston: Little, Brown, 1973, p. 437.

[88]Kenneth R. Pelletier. *Toward a Science of Consciousness*. New York: Dell, 1978, p. 30.

[89]Werner Heisenberg. *Across the Frontiers*. New York: Harper and Row, 1974, p. 68.

[90]Thomas Kuhn. *The Structure of Scientific Revolutions*, 2nd edition. Chicago: University of Chicago Press, 1970.

[91]Willis W. Harman. "The Coming Transformation in Our View of Knowledge," *The Futurist*, Vol. 8, No. 3 (June 1974), pp. 126-128.

[92]Robert E. Lane. "The Decline of Politics and Ideology in a Knowledgeable Society." *American Sociological Review*, Vol. 21, No. 5 (October 1966), p. 650.

[93]Daniel Bell. *The Coming of Post-Industrial Society*. New York: Basic Books, 1973.

[94]Gary Zukav. *The Dancing Wu Li Masters*. New York: Bantam New Age Books, 1979, p. 205.

[95]Fritjof Capra. *The Tao of Physics*. New York: Bantam Books, 1975, p. 42.

[96]"Health." *The Futurist*, Vol. 14, No. 6 (December 1980), p. 75.

[97]David Osborne. "America's Plentiful Energy Resource," *The Atlantic Monthly*, Vol. 253, No. 3 (March, 1984), p. 86.

[98]"What the Next Fifty Years Will Bring," *U.S. News & World Report*, Vol. 94, No. 18 (May 9, 1983), p. A16.

[99]Decker F. Walker. "Reflections on the Educational Potential and Limitations of Microcomputers." *Phi Delta Kappan*, Vol. 65, No. 2 (October 1983), p. 103.

[100]Platt, J. *Perception and Change: Projections for Survival*. Ann Arbor, MI: The University of Michigan Press, 1970, 163.

[101]Lester R. Brown. *The Twenty-Ninth Day*. New York: W. W. Norton, 1978.

[102]Willis W. Harman. *An Incomplete Guide...*, pp. 25-28.

[103]John D. Haas. "Worthwhile Futures: You Can't Get There From Here," *The Link*, Vol. 1, No. 5 (May 1978), pp. 2-3.

[104]John McHale. *World Facts and Trends*. New York: Macmillan, 1972.

[105]Paul Hawken, James Ogilvy, and Peter Schwartz. *Seven Tomorrows*. New York: Bantam Books, 1982, pp. 114-115.

[106]Dwight W. Allen and Christopher Dede. *Creating Better Futures for Education* (mimeo). Norfolk, VA: Old Dominion University, 1979, pp. 6-7.

[107]Gary Walz, Carol Jaslow, Helen Mamarchev, and Beth Fishbane. *Images*. Ann Arbor, MI: ERIC/CAPS, 1980, p. 131.

[108]Theodore J. Gordon. *The Current Methods of Futures Research*. In A. Toffler (ed.), *The Futurists*. New York: Random House, 1971, p. 180.

[109]J. Glenn and Gerry Guy. "Easy ways to help children think about the future," *The Futurist* (August, 1974), p. 187.

[110]M. Folk. "Computers and Educational Futures Research." In M. Marlen & W. L. Ziegler (eds.), *The Potential of Educational Futures*. Worthington, OH: Charles A. Jones, 1972, 41.

[111]J. E. Hill. *How Schools Can Apply Systems Analysis*. Bloomington, IN: Phi Delta Kappa, 1972, p. 15.

[112]*Ibid.*, p. 15.

[113]Willis W. Harman. "Technology and Educational Policy Research." In E. L. Morphet and D. L. Jesser, *Planning for Effective Utilization of Technology in Education*. Denver, CO: Designing Education for the Future, 1968, p. 251.

[114]Theodore J. Gordon. "The Current Methods of Futures Research." In A. Toffler (ed.), *The Futurists* (New York: Random House, 1971), pp. 170-171.

[115]V.C Ferkiss, *Futurology: Promise, Performance, Prospects*. Beverly Hills, CA: Sage Publications, 1977, p. 10.

[116]Richard Bach. *Illusions*. New York: Dell, 1977, p. 60.

[117]Cornish, et al. *op. cit.*, pp. 219-225.

[118]Draper L. Kauffman, Jr. *Futurism and Future Studies*. Washington, DC: National Education Association, 1976, p. 47.

[119]Draper L. Kauffman, Jr. *Teaching the Future*. Palm Springs, CA: ETC Publications, 1976, p. 30.

[120]C. W. Case, and P.A. Olson (eds.). *The Future: Create or Inherit*. Lincoln, NE: University of Nebraska Printing Service, 1974, pp. 53-58.

[121]Robert Fitch and Cordell Svengalis. *Futures Unlimited*. Washington, DC: National Council for the Social Studies, 1979.

[122]U.S. West. "Future Skills." In *High Schools and the Changing Workplace*. Washington, DC: National Academy of Science, 1984.

[123]Bernard C. Hollister and Deane C. Thompson. *Grokking the Future*. Fairfield, NJ: Pflaum/Standard, 1973, p. 166.

[124]Judith C. Hellfach. *Teacher's Guide for Future Studies*. Englewood Cliffs, NJ: Prentice-Hall, 1977, p. 3.

[125]Edward Cornish. "Critical Choices," *The Futurist*. Vol 14, No. 1 (January 1980), pp. 5-13.

[126]Rob Melnick. *Visions of the Future*. Indianapolis: Hudson Institute, 1984.

[127]Elliott Self. "Seven Dimensions of a Future Living Education," *Bulletin of the World Future Society*. Vol. 18, No. 2 (March-April 1984), pp. 7-14.